Susan Grant

T0268550

Getting Started with Cambridge IGCSE® and O Level Economics

CAMBRIDGE
UNIVERSITY PRESS

University Printing House, Cambridge CB2 8BS, United Kingdom

One Liberty Plaza, 20th Floor, New York, NY 10006, USA

477 Williamstown Road, Port Melbourne, VIC 3207, Australia

314–321, 3rd Floor, Plot 3, Splendor Forum, Jasola District Centre, New Delhi – 110025, India

79 Anson Road, #06–04/06, Singapore 079906

Cambridge University Press is part of the University of Cambridge.

It furthers the University's mission by disseminating knowledge in the pursuit of education, learning and research at the highest international levels of excellence.

Information on this title: www.cambridge.org/ 9781108440431

© Cambridge University Press 2018

This publication is in copyright. Subject to statutory exception and to the provisions of relevant collective licensing agreements, no reproduction of any part may take place without the written permission of Cambridge University Press.

First published 2018

20 19 18 17 16 15 14 13 12 11 10 9 8 7 6 5 4 3 2 1

Printed in Malaysia by Vivar Printing

A catalogue record for this publication is available from the British Library

ISBN 978-1-108-44043-1 Paperback

Cambridge University Press has no responsibility for the persistence or accuracy of URLs for external or third-party internet websites referred to in this publication, and does not guarantee that any content on such websites is, or will remain, accurate or appropriate. Information regarding prices, travel timetables, and other factual information given in this work is correct at the time of first printing but Cambridge University Press does not guarantee the accuracy of such information thereafter.

IGCSE® is a registered trademark

All examination-style questions, sample mark schemes, solutions and/or comments that appear in this book were written by the author. In examination, the way marks would be awarded to answers like these may be different.

NOTICE TO TEACHERS IN THE UK
It is illegal to reproduce any part of this work in material form (including photocopying and electronic storage) except under the following circumstances:

(i) where you are abiding by a licence granted to your school or institution by the Copyright Licensing Agency;
(ii) where no such licence exists, or where you wish to exceed the terms of a licence, and you have gained the written permission of Cambridge University Press;
(iii) where you are allowed to reproduce without permission under the provisions of Chapter 3 of the Copyright, Designs and Patents Act 1988, which covers, for example, the reproduction of short passages within certain types of educational anthology and reproduction for the purposes of setting examination questions.

This book, as its name suggests, has been written to give you some idea about what economics involves. In the book you will come across some of the key topics economists examine, discover some key economic terms and concepts, see and draw some key economic diagrams, and start to think as an economist.

Where dollars are referred to in the book, they are US dollars unless otherwise stated.

Section 1 outlines what economics is and some of the benefits of studying economics. It also provides some examples of famous people from a number of countries who have studied economics.

The largest section is Section 2. In this section, the economics linked to 20 topical questions is explored. In each chapter there are a number of activities for you to do, either individually or, more often, as a group. There are also discussion points for you to debate. At the end of each chapter there is a summary, end-of-chapter questions and a suggested independent research task. As its name suggests, the summary mentions the important points covered in the chapter. The end-of-chapter questions ask you about both what you have learned and to build on what you have learned. Some of these questions are quite challenging. The independent research tasks provide you with the opportunity to explore the questions in a little more depth.

Section 3 covers some of the key numbers economists use and some key economic firms, markets and organisations. It also provides brief details of a number of influential economists.

The final section includes suggested answers to the activities in Section 2.

Keeping up-to-date

Economics is an ever-changing subject. Countries' economic performances change, new economic questions arise, governments introduce new economic policies and economists develop new theories about how the economy works. This is why economists have to keep up-to-date with what is happening in the world. To do this, it is important to check the news regularly. You can do this by looking at news websites, such as the *BBC News* website, *The Economic Times* website, or by reading a quality newspaper.

How to use this book

Key terms

These definitions throughout will help you to start learning and understand important terminology and concepts within the field of economics.

KEY TERM

The economy: the country or region in terms of the activities involved in buying, producing and selling products.

Discussion point

Discussion Point features encourage you to think hard about a particular economic issue that has been discussed in the book. Sometimes you will be asked to think about your own opinion on a particular topic, or asked to explore both sides of a debated economic issue.

DISCUSSION POINT

At what age do you think children should start school?

INDIVIDUAL ACTIVITY 1

Identify:

a a private cost arising from people smoking

b an external cost arising from people smoking.

Individual activity

As you work through the book, you will find a series of individual questions and exercises that have been designed to help you check your understanding about concepts and topics that have been introduced in the book.

Group activity

Group activities provide the opportunity for you to engage with your peers, working in pairs or groups to share ideas and exchange viewpoints on a particular economic issue or idea.

GROUP ACTIVITY 1

Select a substitute for each of the following products:

a bus travel

b coffee

c cotton shirts

d orange juice

e peas.

End-of-chapter questions

End-of-chapter questions ask you about what you have learned and offers the opportunity to build on what you have learned. Some of these questions are quite challenging.

End-of-chapter questions

1 What does raising the school leaving age mean?
2 What may be the opportunity cost of someone becoming an art teacher?
3 Why is opportunity cost an important economics concept?
4 Why do you think some children in poor countries leave school at a young age?
5 Why do people who leave school at a later age usually earn more than those who left earlier?
6 Are the friends you may make at school a private or an external benefit?
7 What is social benefit minus private benefits equal to?
8 When a government is deciding whether to raise the school leaving age, should it base its decision on social benefit or private benefits?
9 If ten workers produce output valued at $600 in two hours, what is their productivity?
10 Why do you think productivity has increased in most countries in the past 20 years?

INDEPENDENT RESEARCH

Compare the education system in your country with the education system in another country. For instance, you may want to look at the system by searching on the official website for Sweden. Think about the causes and consequences of the differences.

Independent research

Independent Research tasks provide you with the opportunity to explore topics and questions you have looked at in a little more depth. They often direct you to websites, articles or news stories which link with the concepts you have been learning about.

Summary

In this chapter you have learned that:

- People leave school at different ages in different countries.
- Raising the school leaving age would require more teachers, classrooms and equipment.
- Providing more education will involve an opportunity cost.
- Opportunity cost is the best alternative choice that has been given up.
- Governments, firms, workers and consumers take into account opportunity cost when making their decisions.
- Private benefits are the benefits enjoyed by the people who are buying, or being given a product, and those producing it.
- The private benefits of education enjoyed by students include enjoyment, and higher employment and earning potential.
- External benefits are the benefits enjoyed by those who are not directly involved in producing or consuming a product.
- The external benefits of education include a higher quantity, and quality, of goods and services.
- Social benefit is the total benefit to society. It is private benefits plus external benefits.
- Productivity is the output that a worker can produce in an hour.
- Higher productivity can result from better education, better equipment to work with, training, better working conditions and better healthcare.

Summary

Short, bullet-pointed summaries at the end of chapters in section 2 provide a useful overview of the key learning points introduced in that chapter.

SECTION 1
Introducing economics

Chapter 1
What is economics?

The nature of economics

Economics is about choices and what influences those choices. We, as individuals, have to make choices as to how we spend our time, what we buy and what jobs we do. Firms have to make choices about, for instance, what to produce and governments have to decide how to spend their tax revenue.

In addition to the topics covered in this book, economists are currently studying other key economic ideas such as:

- whether healthcare should be provided free to patients
- why tourism is increasing in China
- whether famines can be eliminated
- how people can be encouraged to eat more healthily
- whether elephants will become extinct
- why some people are homeless.

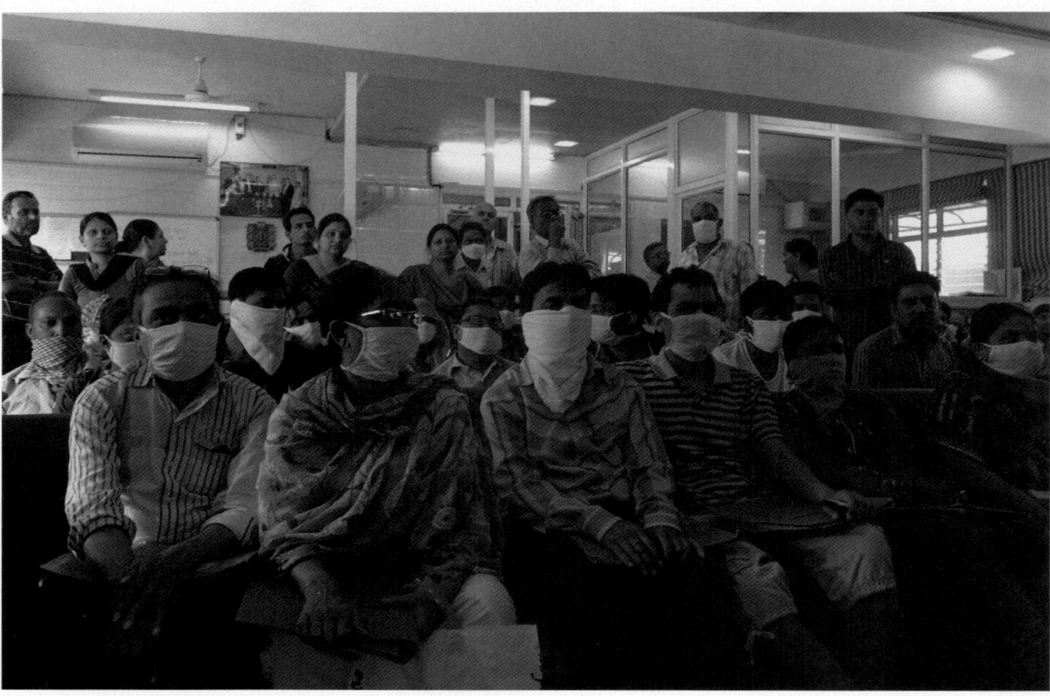

1.1 Should healthcare be provided free to patients?

KEY TERM

The economy: the country or region in terms of the activities involved in buying, producing and selling products.

The tools of economics

Economics has a range of tools to examine how an **economy** works and how its performance can be improved. These include:

- economic terms
- economic concepts

- statistical information
- observations of human behaviour
- economic theories.

Economics is a way of thinking. It encourages everyone who studies it to think logically, examining causes and consequences.

A good economist is someone who is interested in human behaviour and what is happening not only in their own country but also in other countries. She, or he, has a variety of skills, including the ability to:

- write clearly
- examine both sides of an argument
- interpret and use numbers
- draw and interpret diagrams
- explain current issues
- consider the past and make predictions about the future.

The power of economics

Economics has the power to change lives. The ideas of economists and the advice they give to businesses, the government and international organisations can improve the quality of people's lives. Someone born in 1970 could, on average, expect to live to 57. By 2017, this had risen to 72. Over the same period the proportion of children of primary school age not going to school fell from 28% to 8%. People are living longer and more enjoyable lives, in part because of the work of economists.

Economics and medicine

Economics is rather like medicine. Doctors have to learn how a healthy body works, what can go wrong with it and the possible solutions to the problems. Economists explain how an efficient economy would work. They then examine the causes and consequences of economies not working efficiently. They explore economic issues and problems such as poverty, lack of jobs, falling output and prices rising too rapidly. They recommend policy measures to solve or reduce the problems.

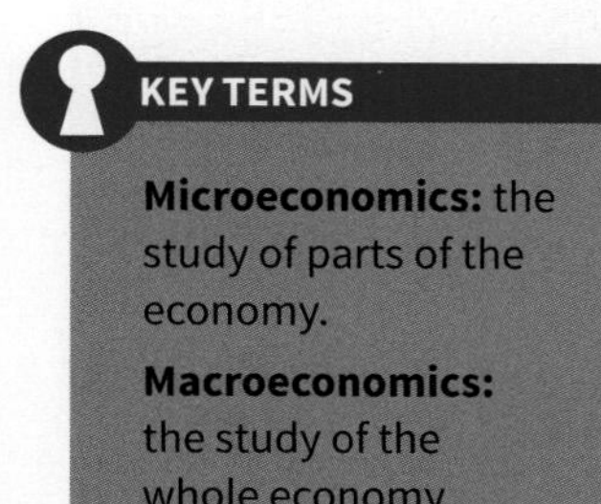

Doctors may choose to specialise in working on part of the body, for instance, performing heart surgery. Other doctors may decide to be family doctors, dealing with the whole body. Similarly, some economists concentrate on **microeconomics**. This is economics on a small scale. It covers topics such as why lawyers are paid more than taxi drivers, what will be the effect of a fall in demand for rice on the price of both rice and other food such as bread, and how changes in technology are affecting the car industry. Other economists specialise in **macroeconomics**. This is economics on a large scale. Among macroeconomic topics are changes in a country's output, changes in the number of people in a country who are in work and why a country may be selling fewer products to other countries.

Chapter 2
The benefits of studying economics

The key benefits

The key benefits that you will gain from studying economics are:

- enjoyment
- being better informed about current issues
- the development of skills that are useful in studying other subjects
- good employment opportunities.

Enjoyment

Economics is a fascinating and challenging subject. It deals with real-world issues in a way that will develop your analytical and evaluative skills. You will have the opportunity to work on your own and in groups. You will engage in class discussions and come to understand that there can be different views on the effects of economic events, and on the causes and solutions to economic problems.

A key piece of evidence that students enjoy economics is that a high proportion of them go on to study economics at university.

2.1 University students

Being better informed about current events

Studying economics will keep you informed about the key influences and events that will affect your and other people's lives. For instance, you may gain an insight into why a factory near you has closed down and how an increase in government spending on healthcare may affect the country. You will be better informed about what is happening in the news than many people. You will be able to distinguish between comments made by journalists and politicians that are based on uninformed, general opinion and those that are based on clear analysis.

The development of skills that are useful in studying other subjects

The skills you will develop studying economics will help you in your other studies. You will learn to write using clear language and structured paragraphs. This should improve your performance in your English lessons. Interpreting statistical tables and carrying out calculations such as percentages will increase your numeracy skills and your performance in mathematics.

KEY TERM

Price elasticity of demand: a measure of how responsive demand is to a change in price.

Some of the topics studied in economics are also covered in business studies. For example, students who have studied **price elasticity of demand** in economics find the topic very straightforward when it is covered in business studies.

To understand current issues, economics students have to be aware of recent history. This can help with studies of modern history. Economics covers trade between different countries and comparisons of different countries' economic performance. These topics may prove useful in your geography studies.

The focus on current issues and the choices that have to be made will also be helpful if you are studying politics or global perspectives.

Good employment opportunities

Employers respect economics as a qualification. This is because it is seen as an academic subject that develops skills that are useful in work. These include the ability to:

- think logically
- assess both sides of an argument
- make informed judgements
- present information in a variety of forms
- write clear reports
- work in teams.

Some students who have studied economics go on to become economists. They work for businesses, banks, the government and universities.

Other students get a variety of jobs including as chief executives, lawyers, accountants and journalists. The next chapter gives some examples of the jobs that some famous people who studied economics at university are undertaking.

Chapter 3
Famous people who have studied economics

Cate Blanchett is a world famous actress who has appeared in films such as *Elizabeth* and *Thor*. She studied economics at Melbourne University, Australia.

Ana Patricia Botin is a Spanish banker. She is the executive chairwoman of the Santander Banking group. She gained an economics degree from Bryn Mawr College, USA.

Warren Buffett is one of the world's richest financial investors and chief executives. He has an economics degree from Columbia School of Business, USA.

Mick Jagger is the lead singer with the music group the Rolling Stones. He studied economics, economic history and politics at the London School of Economics, UK.

Arianna Huffington is the co-founder and editor in chief of the *Huffington Post*. She studied economics at Cambridge University, UK.

Sri Mulyani Indrawati is an Indonesian economist. She has been the managing director of the World Bank and Indonesia's Finance Minister. She has a degree in economics from the University of Illinois, USA.

Imran Khan is a former international cricketer and politician in Pakistan. He has a degree in philosophy, politics and economics from Oxford University, UK.

Shah Rukh Kahn is a famous Indian actor and film producer. He studied economics at Hansraj College, India.

Thabo Mbeki was president of South Africa from 1999 to 2008. He studied economics at Sussex University, UK.

Elon Musk is an entrepreneur and inventor. He studied economics at Wharton School of Business, USA.

Sheryl Sandberg became the chief operating officer of Facebook in 2008. She also started Lean In, an organisation which encourages women to learn new skills and which promotes women's rights. She studied economics at Harvard University, USA.

Manmohan Singh is an economist and politician. Among his qualifications, he gained a PhD in economics from Oxford University, UK. He was Prime Minister of India from 2004 to 2014.

Arsene Wenger was manager of Arsenal football club in the UK from 1996 to 2018. He gained a degree in economics and politics from Strasbourg University, France.

Zhang Xin is head of the largest commercial property developer in Beijing. She has economics degrees from Sussex and Cambridge Universities, UK.

Janet Yellen is an economist. She was head of the Federal Reserve, the US central bank from 2014 to 2018. She studied economics at Brown University and Harvard University, USA.

SECTION 2
Key economic ideas

Chapter 4
Should the school leaving age be raised?

Differences in the school leaving age

KEY TERM

Adult literacy rate: the proportion of people aged 15 and above who can read and write.

Do you know when you will leave school? Carlos de Rosas, an 18-year-old from Argentina has just left school. He is going on to study economics at the National University of La Plata. In contrast, Maurice Yarga has just left school at nine, having gone to primary school for only two years. He is going to work on his family's small cotton farm. Maurice lives in the West African country of Burkina Faso. Average income in the country is very low. Attendance at school is supposed to be compulsory from age seven to age 14. In practice, however, attendance is not enforced. The country has the world's lowest **adult literacy rate** with only 26% of adults being able to read and write. Maurice cannot read or write and this will affect his future employment opportunities and the quality of his life.

4.1 A young person working on a farm in Burkina Faso

INDIVIDUAL AND GROUP ACTIVITY 1

a Individually, find out at what age your parents and grandparents left school.

b Share your findings with others in the group and discuss whether you are likely to leave school at an older or younger age than your parents and grandparents.

Raising the school leaving age

Many governments now enforce an age that students have to reach before they can leave full-time education. A number of these governments have raised or are planning to raise the school leaving age. If students are going to study for longer, there will need to be:

- more teachers
- more classrooms
- more books
- more computers.

All of these cost money. For instance, in 2017 the cost of employing 300 more teachers in Burkina Faso would have been 1.125 billion West African francs.

Opportunity cost

This 1.125 billion West African francs seems like a very large sum of money. It is unlikely, however, that you know what 1.125 billion West African francs is worth in your own currency. You are also unlikely to know what that amount of money could buy in Burkina Faso in 2017. You might suggest that the government of Burkina Faso should not employ more teachers as it seems very expensive. You may then find out it would actually be relatively cheap.

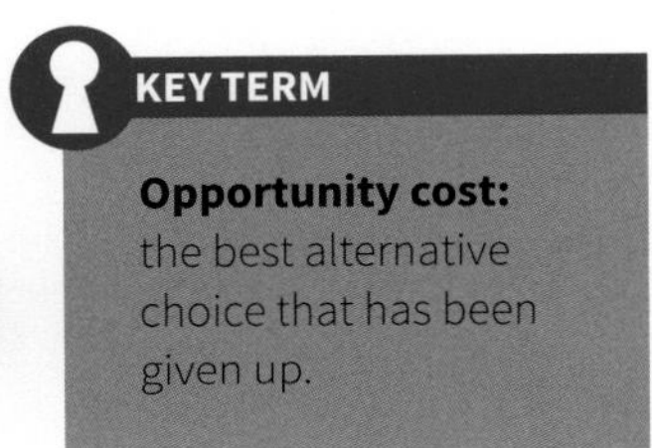

KEY TERM

Opportunity cost: the best alternative choice that has been given up.

To make informed choices, economists make use of a concept known as **opportunity cost**. As its name suggests, this is a cost based on what opportunity has been lost by making a particular choice. For instance, there will be a range of things that the government of Burkina Faso could spend more money on. These may also include treating more patients in state-run hospitals, building more homes for the poor, building more roads and constructing more public parks. The government is likely to narrow these choices down to two – its two most favoured choices. These may be to raise the school leaving age or to treat more patients. In this case, if the government decides to raise the school leaving age, it is giving up its next best choice – the opportunity to treat more patients. So the opportunity cost of raising the school leaving age is treating more patients.

KEY TERMS

Firms: business concerns that produce goods and services.

Consumers: those who obtain products for their own use. They may buy them or receive them free.

The significance of opportunity cost

In making a decision, it is important to consider the cost in terms of the best alternative choice that could have been made. This will bring out what it really costs in a meaningful way.

As well as governments, **firms** make choices about what to produce. Workers also make choices about what jobs to do and **consumers** make choices about what to buy. In making such choices, it is important that options are considered to ensure that we make the choices that are right for us.

GROUP ACTIVITY 2

In your group, decide what may have been the opportunity cost in each case:

a a student's decision to study A-Level Economics

b a family's decision to go on holiday to Sri Lanka

c a person's decision to become an accountant

d a publishing firm's decision to print more history books

e a government's decision to spend more on defence.

KEY TERMS

Private benefits: benefits enjoyed by those directly consuming or producing a product.

External benefits: benefits enjoyed by those not directly involved in the consumption and production activities of others.

Social benefit: the total benefit to a society of an economic activity.

Why may a government decide to raise the school leaving age?

A government may think that the benefits of raising the school leaving age are considerable. It may think that these benefits will be greater than those that can be gained from other options. What may these benefits be? There are a number. They can be divided into two types:

- One is the benefits that may be enjoyed by the students themselves. These benefits, are known to economists as **private benefits**. They may include enjoyment from studying, a greater choice of occupation and higher earnings.
- The second type of benefits are those that may be gained by other people. These people are the people who are not involved in education. They are not students or teachers. If you are better educated, other people in your country may be able to enjoy more, and better, quality goods and services. Economists call this type of benefits **external benefits**.

The total benefit that society would gain from raising the school leaving age is called the **social benefit**. It consists of both the external and private benefits.

DISCUSSION POINT

At what age do you think children should start school?

GROUP ACTIVITY 3

In your group, divide the following into the private and the external benefits of increased government spending on healthcare:

a an increase in the pay of nurses

b an increase in the quality of food produced as farm workers will be healthier

c a reduction in the time between diagnosis and treatment of patients

d a reduction in the loss of pay as workers will have less time off work

e a reduction in the chance of others catching infectious diseases.

A higher school leaving age and productivity

KEY TERM

Productivity: output per worker hour.

Better educated people become better workers. In most cases, they produce more goods and services for every hour they work. They are said to have higher **productivity**. For example, a well-educated worker in an insurance firm may be able to process four insurance claims in an hour. A less-educated worker may be able to process only two insurance claims an hour. Increasing the productivity of workers enables people to enjoy more goods and services.

Apart from more education, what else can cause productivity to rise? There are a number of other possible causes including:

- workers having better equipment to work with
- training given to workers on the job
- higher pay may encourage workers to work harder
- better working conditions can make it easier for workers to do their job
- better healthcare should make workers fitter, more energetic and capable of greater concentration.

DISCUSSION POINT

What do you think should be the school leaving age in your country?

Summary

In this chapter you have learned that:

- People leave school at different ages in different countries.
- Raising the school leaving age would require more teachers, classrooms and equipment.
- Providing more education will involve an opportunity cost.
- Opportunity cost is the best alternative choice that has been given up.
- Governments, firms, workers and consumers take into account opportunity cost when making their decisions.
- Private benefits are the benefits enjoyed by the people who are buying, or being given a product, and those producing it.
- The private benefits of education enjoyed by students include enjoyment, and higher employment and earning potential.
- External benefits are the benefits enjoyed by those who are not directly involved in producing or consuming a product.
- The external benefits of education include a higher quantity, and quality, of goods and services.
- Social benefit is the total benefit to society. It is private benefits plus external benefits.
- Productivity is the output that a worker can produce in an hour.
- Higher productivity can result from better education, better equipment to work with, training, better working conditions and better healthcare.

End-of-chapter questions

1 What does raising the school leaving age mean?

2 What may be the opportunity cost of someone becoming an art teacher?

3 Why is opportunity cost an important economics concept?

4 Why do you think some children in poor countries leave school at a young age?

5 Why do people who leave school at a later age usually earn more than those who left earlier?

6 Are the friends you may make at school a private or an external benefit?

7 What is social benefit minus private benefits equal to?

8 When a government is deciding whether to raise the school leaving age, should it base its decision on social benefit or private benefits?

9 If ten workers produce output valued at $600 in two hours, what is their productivity?

10 Why do you think productivity has increased in most countries in the past 20 years?

INDEPENDENT RESEARCH

Compare the education system in your country with the education system in another country. For instance, you may want to look at the system by searching on the official website for Sweden. Think about the causes and consequences of the differences.

Chapter 5
Why are some brands of trainers (sneakers) so expensive?

The desire for branded trainers

Avinash Bachoo lives in Tamarin, a village on the west coast of Mauritius. He needs a new pair of trainers. His mother is trying to persuade him to accept a pair of non-branded trainers that are selling for 680 Mauritian rupees (approximately $20). Avinash, however, saw a tourist wearing a pair of branded trainers he would really like to have. He noticed these for sale in a shop in Port Louis, the country's capital. These trainers are priced at 3250 Mauritian rupees ($95).

Differences in the price of trainers

Some designer trainers, those with the most famous brand names, are more expensive than non-branded trainers. Why is this? It is because they are more popular. Economists talk about them being in higher **demand**. There are people willing and able to pay high prices for certain brands. They are willing to buy them because they are attracted to the trainers by their look and name. Advertising is widely used to make the trainers desirable and appear unique. The ability to buy a product is determined by the amount of money people have. Some people may want designer trainers but they may not be able to afford them.

KEY TERM

Demand: the willingness and ability to buy a product.

5.1 Display of branded trainers in a store

The effect of a fall in price

If the price of designer trainers falls, it is likely that more pairs will be bought. This is because more people will be able to afford them and they may appear to be of better value than rival brands.

Demand schedules and demand curves

Economists produce **demand schedules** and **demand curves**. These show how many units of a product will be demanded at different prices. Table 5.1 shows how many pairs of a particular brand of trainers people would demand a week at different prices.

Table 5.1 A demand schedule for Windrush trainers per week

Price $	Pairs of trainers demanded (thousands)
60	20
55	26
50	35
45	48
40	63
35	85

KEY TERMS

Demand schedule: a table that shows the different quantities of a product that would be demanded at different prices.

Demand curve: a graph that shows the relationship between the price and the quantity demanded of a product.

This information can also be shown on a demand curve – see Figure 5.1. Such a curve measures price on the vertical (upwards line) axis and the quantity demanded on the horizontal axis (the line that runs across from left to right).

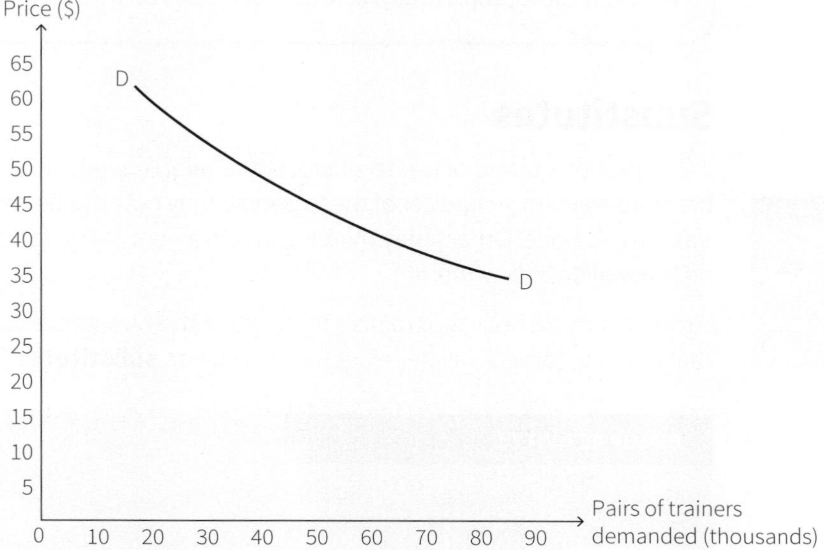

Fig. 5.1 The demand curve for Windrush trainers

INDIVIDUAL ACTIVITY 1

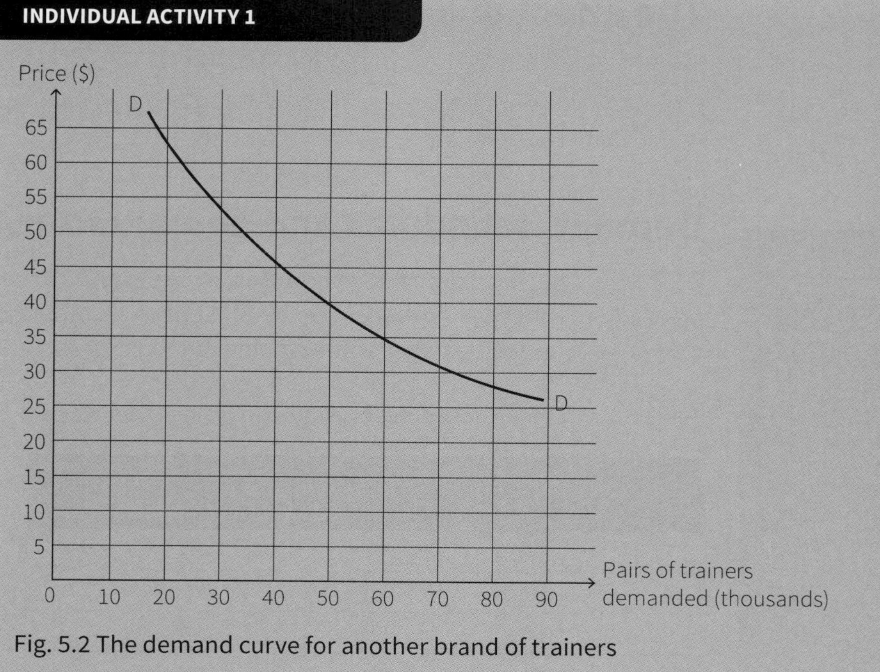

Fig. 5.2 The demand curve for another brand of trainers

Using the demand curve in Fig. 5.2:

a How many pairs of trainers are demanded at a price of $50?

b if the firm wants to sell 50 pairs of trainers, what price should it charge?

DISCUSSION POINT

What may cause people to buy more pairs of trainers even if their price has not changed?

Substitutes

KEY TERM

Substitute: a product that can be used in place of another.

If the price of a brand of trainers rises, some people switch to other brands and to non-branded trainers. A number of these people may now not be able to afford the brand that has risen in price. Others may think that the trainers are no longer worth the price. They will be less willing to buy them.

Firms that make branded trainers try to make their trainers as unique as possible. This is so that their customers will be reluctant to switch to **substitutes**.

GROUP ACTIVITY 1

Select a substitute for each of the following products:

a bus travel

b coffee

c cotton shirts

d orange juice

e peas.

KEY TERM

Profit: the positive difference between revenue and cost.

Profit

Whereas buyers want low prices, firms that sell trainers want high prices. Firms have to cover the cost of making the trainers and they want to make a **profit**. The more people are prepared to buy, the more firms are likely to be able and willing to sell.

KEY TERMS

Supply schedule: a table that shows the relationship between price and the quantity supplied of a product.

Supply curve: a graph that shows the relationship between the price and the quantity supplied of a product.

Supply: the willingness and ability to sell a product.

Supply schedules and curves

As well as demand schedules and demand curves, economists also produce **supply schedules** and **supply curves**. The difference with **supply** is that price and supply move in the same direction. A rise in price will cause firms to supply more. Table 5.2 shows the supply schedule for Windrush trainers.

Table 5.2 A supply schedule for Windrush trainers per week

Price $	Pairs of trainers supplied (thousands)
60	96
55	75
50	60
45	48
40	39
35	34

The information can be plotted on a supply curve as shown in Figure 5.3.

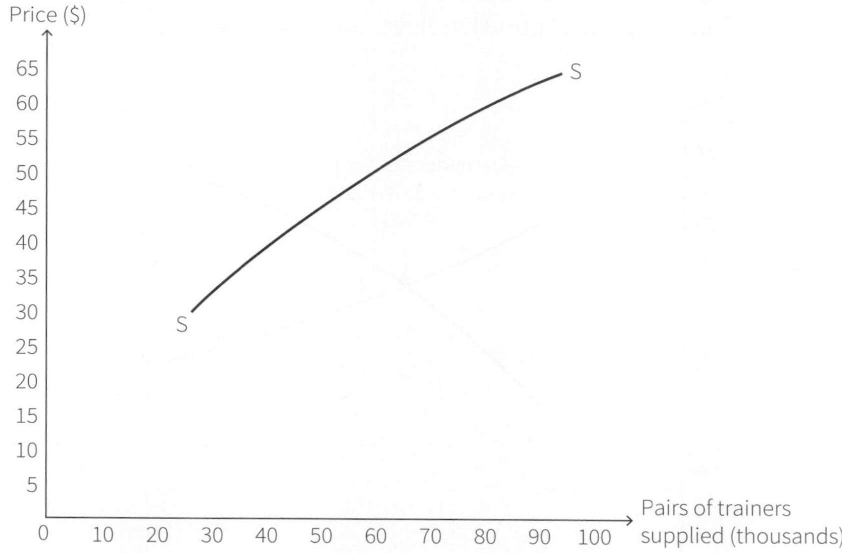

Fig. 5.3 The supply curve for Windrush trainers

INDIVIDUAL ACTIVITY 2

From the supply schedule for Fleet trainers per week (Table 5.3), plot the supply curve.

Table 5.3 A supply schedule for Fleet trainers per week

Price $	Pairs of trainers supplied (thousands)
60	120
55	95
50	66
45	44
40	28
35	19

Price

If buyers want low prices and firms want higher prices, what prices will be charged? In practice, firms may try out a number of prices. If firms find that they cannot sell all the trainers they want to at a particular price, they are likely to lower the price. In contrast, they are likely to raise the price if the number of trainers people are demanding is higher than the trainers they have available to sell. When they find that demand is equal to their supply, they are likely to leave price unchanged.

So the price charged takes into account both the amount buyers are willing to pay and the amount that firms are willing and able to accept. Economists combine the demand and supply curves to illustrate how price is determined. Figure 5.4 shows how the demand for and supply of the Windrush trainers is equal at $45.

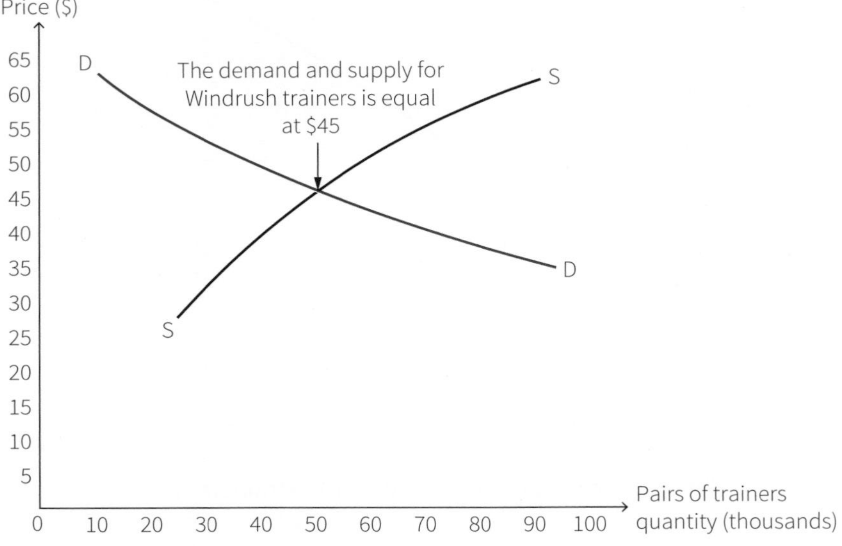

Fig. 5.4 The market for Windrush trainers

Demand and supply diagrams are probably the most famous type of diagrams used by economists.

DISCUSSION POINT

Discuss whether you think the price of a particular brand of trainers sold in your country will increase in the future.

Summary

In this chapter you have learned that:

- Branded products are usually more expensive than non-branded products.
- People are attracted to designer trainers but not everyone can afford them.
- If the price of a product falls, people are likely to be more willing and more able to buy it.
- Economists show the relationship between price and demand using demand schedules and demand curves.
- A demand curve slopes down from left to right, showing that a rise in price causes a fall in demand, and vice versa.
- A rise in price may cause some consumers to switch to substitutes.
- Supply schedules and supply curves show how much firms will sell at different prices.
- A supply curve slopes up from left to right. This shows that a rise in price will cause a rise in supply.
- The price charged for a product tends to move to where demand and supply are equal.

End-of-chapter questions

1 What makes branded products so popular?

2 What influences people's ability to buy a product?

3 How are substitutes linked to people's willingness to buy a product?

4 What is shown on a demand schedule?

5 What effect will a rise in price have on demand?

6 What are the differences between demand and supply?

7 What is on the vertical axis of demand and supply diagrams?

8 What motivates firms to supply goods and services?

9 Why does a rise in price make firms more able to supply trainers?

10 What will happen to the price of trainers if shops are running out of trainers to sell?

INDEPENDENT RESEARCH

Find out the price of a pair of branded trainers in your country. Compare it with the price of other trainers in your country and with the same pair in another country. Think about what might explain these differences.

Chapter 6
Why do some footballers earn more than $30 million a year?

The popularity of football

Football is played throughout the world. It continues to increase in popularity. Tang Li Min and her parents try to watch every home game, and some away games of Shanghai SIPG football club, which plays in the Chinese Super League. The club, known by fans as the Red Eagles, earned more than $40 million revenue in 2017. Across the world in Buenos Aires in Argentina, Carlos Garcia, a 16-year-old, plays for the youth side of a local team. He hopes to progress to the first team and to do as well as another former citizen of Buenos Aires, Diego Maradona. In Southampton in England, Megan Collet, who plays for Southampton Football Club's under-14 girls team, dreams of playing professional football.

Highly-paid footballers

Some football players are very well paid. In 2017, a number of footballers earned more than $30 million a year, with at least one footballer earning more than $50 million. This was the Brazilian Neymar, who signed for Paris Saint-Germain, a French football club for a transfer fee of around $263 million. He became the world's highest-paid football player.

The highest-paid footballers receive money from a number of sources. Most get paid a wage from their clubs, plus bonuses if their teams are successful. They also earn money from, for example, appearing in advertisements and endorsing a range of products including football boots and clothing.

Why do some football clubs pay their players so much?

The top football clubs pay their footballers high wages because of the revenue they can get from employing them. Skilled players can result in their team doing well. Doing well in the top leagues can attract large crowds to watch the team in the stadium. It can also result in the club selling TV rights and merchandise such as replica shirts.

The people who have the skills to play football at the top level are in short supply. Players such as Neymar are offered high wages because football clubs are competing to sign them.

DISCUSSION POINT

Would Manchester United's first team players leave the club if they were paid less money?

GROUP ACTIVITY 1

In your group, decide whether the following changes would be likely to increase or reduce the wages of footballers playing for the Spanish club, Real Madrid:

a a rise in the fees paid by TV programmes for covering Real Madrid games
b relegation of the team to a lower division
c the opening of a new larger stadium
d an increase in the popularity of watching other sports
e an increase in the number of people living in Madrid.

Low pay

Most people work for much lower wages than Neymar. Why is this? In most cases, people have no choice. They may want to be paid more but the jobs they can get are less well-paid. Some people may not have the skills and the qualifications to get high-paid jobs. They may be doing jobs where demand for their services is relatively low. At the same time, the supply of workers for these jobs may be high as many people may be able to do these jobs. Figure 6.1 shows how demand and supply of street cleaners results in lower wages than that of top footballers.

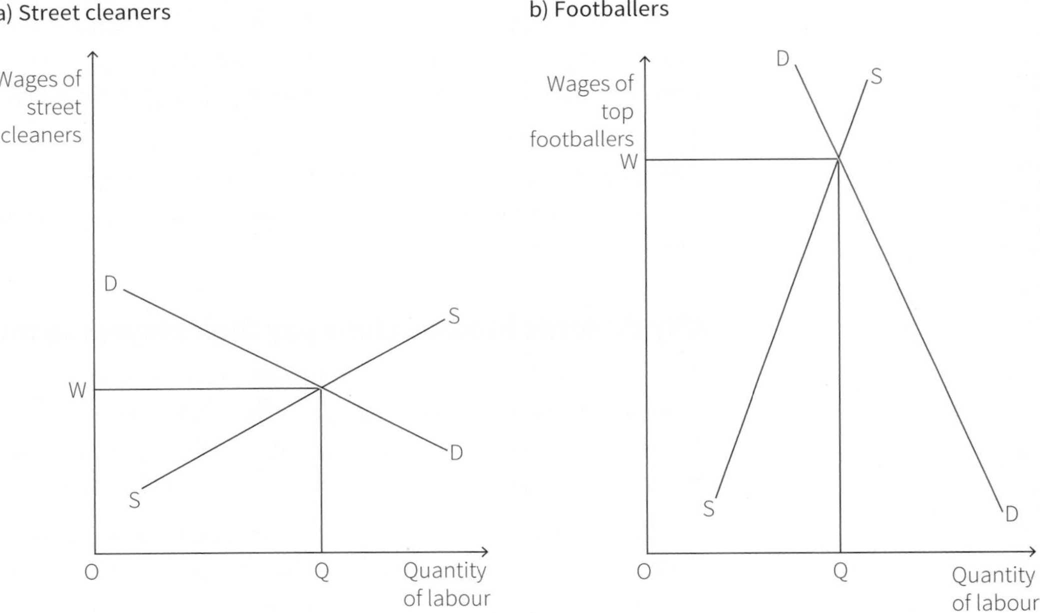

Fig. 6.1 The markets for street cleaners and footballers

Some people may have the skills and qualifications to do high-paid jobs but they may choose to do low-paid jobs. This is because people think about more than just the wages they will receive when they are considering what jobs to do. They consider, for example:

- working hours
- holidays

- promotion chances
- training provided
- nearness to home
- pension provided
- job satisfaction.

KEY TERM

Wage differential: differences in the wages received by different groups of workers.

Wage differentials

In most countries, doctors are paid more than construction workers. Some people may not want to work on building sites. This is because the work can be dirty and dangerous, and involves a degree of physical strength. Despite this, there are more people with the skills to be construction workers than to be doctors. Demand for doctors is high relative to supply. Not many people have the qualifications or the skills needed to be a doctor. Students need to gain high A-Levels to go to university to study medicine. They have to spend time training in hospitals before they are fully qualified.

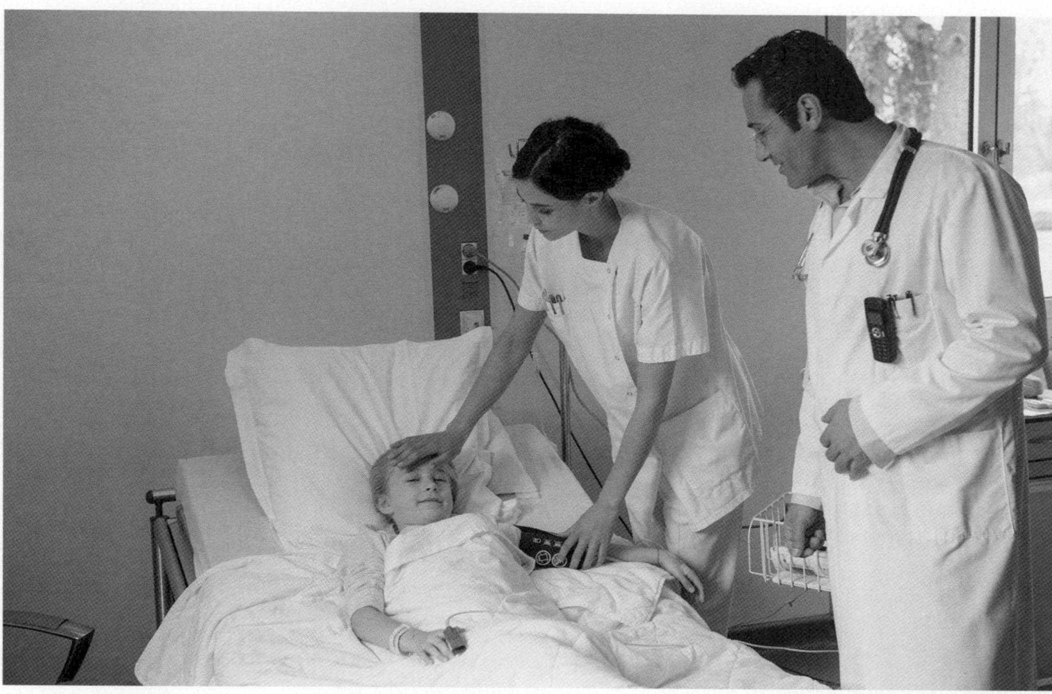

6.1 A doctor and nurse look after a young patient at a hospital

GROUP ACTIVITY 2

Decide in each case which group of workers is likely to be higher paid and why:

a head teachers and teachers
b lawyers and bus drivers
c window cleaners and architects
d hotel cleaners and TV presenters
e opticians and tea pickers.

Why do wages change?

Over time, the wages of most workers increase. Some do, however, fall and some rise more slowly. What causes these changes? There are a number of reasons. The reasons for a rise in wages, for instance, can be put into three groups – increases in demand, decreases in supply and other causes.

Increases in demand

Demand for workers in a particular occupation may increase due to:

- A rise in demand for the product they produce. For instance, the wages of web designers has increased in many countries. This is because more firms and organisations want to have websites and to have high-quality websites.
- A rise in their productivity. If, for instance, car workers can produce more cars per hour, the firms that employ them will earn more money.

Decreases in supply

Supply of a group of workers may decrease due to:

- A rise in the qualifications required to do the job. For instance, it was announced in 2016 that all new police officers in England and Wales would have to be educated to university level by 2020.
- An increase in the length of training on the job. People may be more reluctant to become a doctor, for instance, if it takes longer to become fully qualified.
- A decline in working conditions. If, for instance, a job becomes more dangerous, fewer people would want to do it. For example, if coal miners are required to explore deeper and less stable mines, some miners may decide to leave their jobs.

KEY TERMS

Trade union: an association of workers that represents their interests, and seeks to improve their pay and working conditions.

Industrial action: workers disrupting production to put pressure on employers to agree to their demands.

National minimum wage: a minimum wage rate for an hour's work, fixed by the government for the whole economy.

Other causes

These include:

- An increase in the bargaining power of the workers. A group of workers may join a **trade union**. This organisation will represent them in negotiations with employers for higher wages and better working conditions. The trade union may threaten to take **industrial action**, including strikes, in support of their claims.
- Government policy. A government may raise the wages of low-paid workers by introducing or increasing a **national minimum wage**. A national minimum wage is the lowest wage that employers are allowed to pay their workers. Before the introduction of a national minimum wage, an employer may have been paying its workers $2 an hour. If the government introduces a national minimum wage of $5 an hour, the employer would have to raise the wage rate by at least $3 an hour.

INDIVIDUAL ACTIVITY 1

Copy and complete Table 6.1 by deciding, in each case, whether the changes would increase or decrease the wages of the particular occupation and the reasons why.

Table 6.1

Occupation	Change	Increase/decrease in wages and reason why
Construction workers	A rise in population	
Cricket players	TV channels increasing their coverage of cricket matches	
Dentists	An increase in the training period to become a dentist	
Shop assistants	More people shopping online	
Taxi drivers	The introduction of driverless cars	
University lecturers	More students going to university	

DISCUSSION POINT

Discuss whether you would rather get a job as a teacher or as an accountant and the reasons why.

Summary

In this chapter you have learned that:

- Some footballers are well-paid because they are in high demand and in short supply. They generate high incomes for their clubs and advertising sponsors, and not many people are able to play football to such high standards.
- The demand for workers who have high qualifications and who are skilled is usually greater than the demand for unqualified and unskilled workers.
- Workers are likely to be low paid if demand for their services is low while there is a high number of workers offering these services.
- Workers base their decisions on what jobs they do, not just on the wages offered. They also consider other factors including working hours, holidays, promotion chances, training provided, nearness to home, whether any pension is provided and job satisfaction.
- The wages of workers in a particular occupation will increase if demand for their labour increases and there are fewer people willing and able to do their job.
- Trade unions may succeed in raising the wages their members receive.
- The introduction or increase in a national minimum wage may raise the wages of low-paid workers.

End-of-chapter questions

1. Why are football players who play for clubs in the lower league of Italian football, Serie D, paid less than those in the top league, Serie A?
2. Why are jobs that require high qualifications usually paid more than those that require low or no qualifications?
3. What are the key influences on the demand for a worker?
4. Why are nurses in some countries willing to work for relatively low pay?
5. What effect is a cut in the holidays provided by an employer likely to have on the supply of labour to that job?
6. What are **two** ways a farmer could encourage more people to work on his farm?
7. What effect may an increase in the pay of teachers have on the supply of university lecturers?
8. What may happen to the wages of doctors should more students study medicine at university?
9. Why do some workers join trade unions?
10. Who is a national minimum wage designed to help?

INDEPENDENT RESEARCH

Research how the wages in a particular occupation in your country have changed in recent years. For example, the newspaper article 'Teacher's pay in England down by 12% in 10 years' (*The Guardian*, 12 September 2017) examines changes in the pay of teachers in England in recent years. You can search for the article on the official website for *The Guardian*.

Chapter 7
Why are some people poor?

Poverty today

Adama Keita is 13. He lives in Mali, a country in West Africa. He was born underweight. He is still underweight and is short for his age. He had two brothers but they died at the ages of one and three due to a lack of good-quality food. His parents died from cholera when Adama was eight. Cholera is an infectious disease that can be caught by drinking unclean water. Adama now sleeps under a bridge in the country's capital of Bamako. He begs for money and has never been to school.

Lisa Miller is 15-years-old. She lives in Georgetown, Alabama. The state of Alabama has the fourth highest poverty rate in the USA. Both of Lisa's parents used to work in a supermarket. They lost their jobs three years ago. They have not found other jobs. The family have had to move into cramped, rented accommodation. The government gives the family unemployment benefit and food stamps. These benefits came to $15 000 a year in 2016. The average household income in the same year in the USA was $58 000. Lisa does not have a smartphone or a computer. She expects to leave school soon to search for a job. Unlike some of her fellow students, she will not be going to university.

KEY TERMS

Absolute poverty: a condition where people's income is too low to enable them to meet their basic needs.

Relative poverty: a condition where people are poor in comparison to others in the country. Their income is too low to enable them to enjoy the average standard of living in the country.

What does it mean to be poor?

Some people lack the basic goods needed to survive. They do not have enough income to buy adequate housing, clothing and food. They are in **absolute poverty**. Adama is experiencing absolute poverty.

Relative poverty takes into account the country people live in and the time they live. People are said to be relatively poor when they cannot achieve a minimum standard of living. They cannot take part in the usual activities of the society they live in. Lisa is experiencing relative poverty.

GROUP ACTIVITY 1

a Make a list of what goods and services you would need each day to survive. Research the prices of these products. Total these prices and you will have found a poverty line. People living on an income below this figure may be said to be living in absolute poverty.

b Decide whether someone in absolute poverty is also in relative poverty.

c Using the pictograms on the next page, decide in which two countries a household is most likely to feel relatively poor, if they do not own a car and TV and do not have internet access.

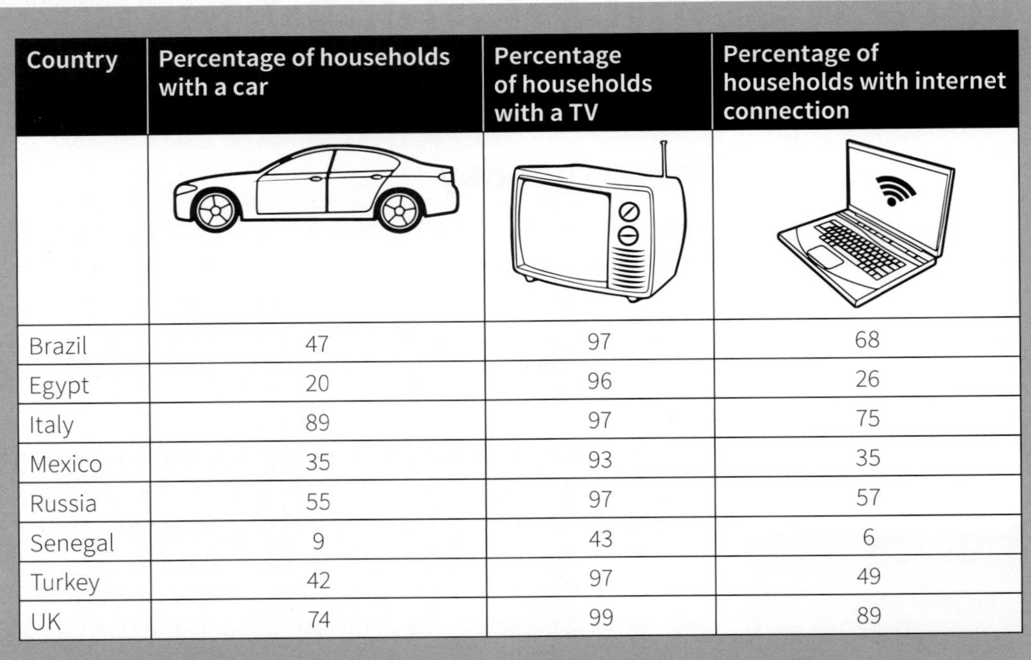

Country	Percentage of households with a car	Percentage of households with a TV	Percentage of households with internet connection
Brazil	47	97	68
Egypt	20	96	26
Italy	89	97	75
Mexico	35	93	35
Russia	55	97	57
Senegal	9	43	6
Turkey	42	97	49
UK	74	99	89

Who are the poor?

There are certain groups that have a higher than average chance of being poor. These include:

- the old
- the sick
- those lacking education
- those discriminated against.

The old and the sick may not be able to work. They may also not have enough savings to buy the goods and services they need. Those lacking education and those who are discriminated against may find it difficult to find employment. Even if they are successful in getting a job, it may be a low-paid one.

DISCUSSION POINT

Why are people who only receive a few years' education likely to be poorer than those with university degrees?

Why is it important to reduce poverty?

Reducing poverty:

- improves the quality of people's lives
- enables people to live longer
- increases the chances of the children of the poor not being poor.

INDIVIDUAL ACTIVITY 1

Using Figure 7.1:

a calculate the difference in life expectancy between Japan and Swaziland

b using the World Factbook – which can be searched for at www.cia.gov – find out the average income (GDP per head) in the six countries shown. Are their incomes in the order that their life expectancies suggest?

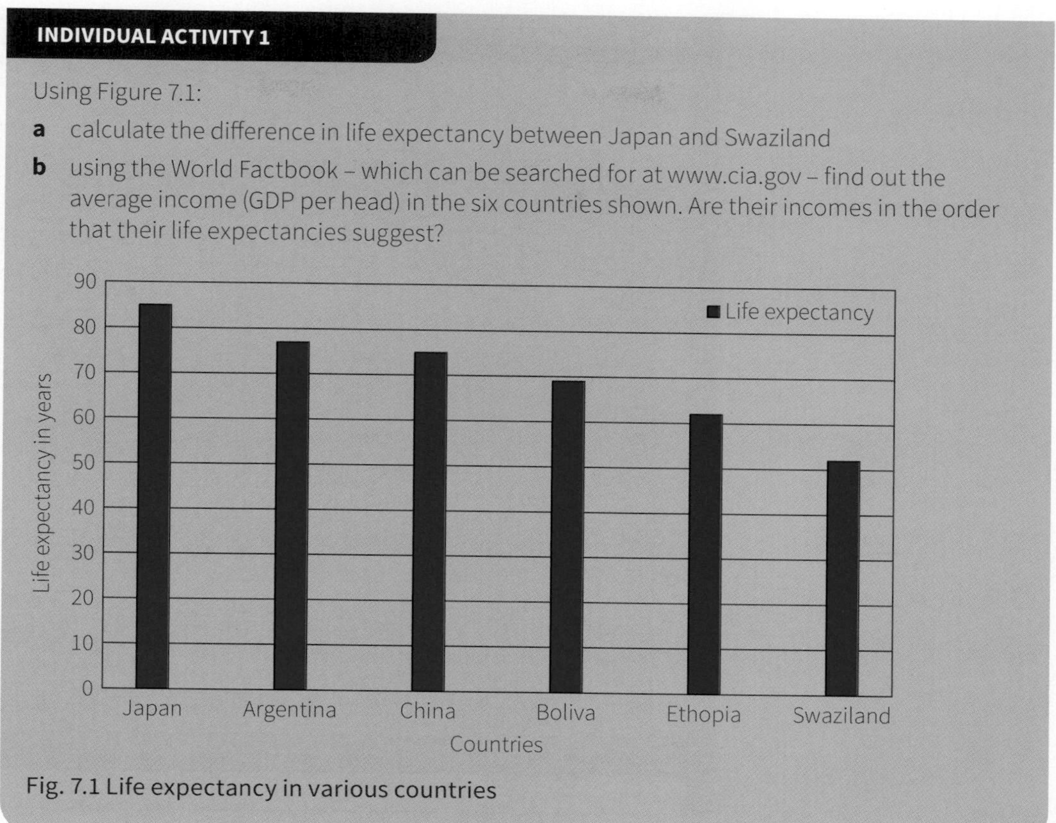

Fig. 7.1 Life expectancy in various countries

GROUP ACTIVITY 2

Produce a list of four reasons why the children of the poor are often poor.

Ways to reduce poverty

Economists suggest a number of ways to reduce poverty. These include:

- Giving money to the old and the sick. This can mean that they have enough money to buy goods and services.
- Improving healthcare. If people are healthy, they are less likely to have time off work. They may also be able to work for longer hours.
- Improving education. More years of better quality education can increase people's skills. Better skilled people have more chances of gaining well-paid jobs.
- Promoting employment. Providing more employment opportunities will give more people opportunity to earn an income.
- Passing laws to end discrimination. Stopping discrimination may mean that groups are paid equally for the same work and have similar chances of being employed.

GROUP ACTIVITY 3

Find out whether the government of your country provides payments (pensions) to retired people and if so how much.

GROUP ACTIVITY 4

Table 7.1 provides some information on two countries. Germany is a country in Western Europe. Malawi is a country in Southeast Africa.

7.1 Bicycle taxi drivers in Malawi waiting for passengers who cannot afford to travel any other way

Table 7.1 Selected data on Germany and Malawi

	Germany	Malawi
Average income	$49 000	$1200
Average years of schooling	17 years	11 years
Life expectancy	80.7 years	61.2 years
Percentage of children under the age of 5 years who are underweight	1.1	13.8
Percentage of households with access to clean drinking water	100	21

a Using the information in Table 7.1, explain why poverty is more of a problem in Malawi than in Germany.

b Discuss whether everyone in Malawi is likely to be poorer than everyone in Germany.

Progress

Poverty is a serious problem but the situation is improving. Fewer people are hungry, life expectancy is increasing and a higher proportion of children are going to school. The World Bank (see Chapter 25) estimated that one in three people in the world were poor in 1995. By 2016, it estimated that one in ten was poor. This figure represents an improvement but still provides a challenge for economists and governments.

DISCUSSION POINT

Do you enjoy a better quality of life than your parents did when they were your age?

Summary

In this chapter you have learned that:

- Some people are poor in rich countries as well as in poor countries.
- People who are in absolute poverty lack basic necessities.
- People are in relative poverty when they cannot fully participate in the activities of society. They are poor, relative to other people in their country.
- The old, the sick, those lacking education, and those discriminated against, may find it difficult to get an income and so may be poor.
- Reducing poverty improves the quality of people's lives.
- Among the ways of reducing poverty are giving money to the old and sick, improving healthcare and education, providing employment and passing laws to end discrimination.
- Levels of poverty vary between countries.
- Poverty is a serious problem, but a smaller proportion of the global population is living in poverty than in the past.

End-of-chapter questions

1 Is everyone poor in a poor country?

2 If someone is in absolute poverty, what basic necessities may they lack?

3 If the income of a person remains unchanged, what would cause them to experience relative poverty?

4 Why do the rich, on average, live longer than the poor?

5 Why may the old be poor?

6 Why are those who have no qualifications more likely to be poor than those with qualifications?

7 How may improving healthcare help to reduce poverty?

8 How may discrimination cause poverty?

9 Are people who are in relative poverty always in absolute poverty?

10 Why do governments try to reduce poverty?

INDEPENDENT RESEARCH

Using the 'Economy' section of the World Factbook (published by the CIA) for your country, find out what percentage of your country's population lives below the poverty line. Navigate to the CIA website and use the search feature to find information.

Then compare this with the percentage in five other countries. You can find a list of the world's populations below the poverty line by clicking on the icon to the right of the heading 'Population below poverty line' in the 'Economy' section of your country. Or you can visit the pages of the individual countries to find the information.

Saving in different countries

Li Mingzhu and her family live in Hangzhou in China. They live in a nice apartment even though they are not a rich family and the price of housing is high in the city. Her parents saved for some time and received help from Mingzhu's grandparents to buy the apartment. Mingzhu's parents are now saving, in part, so that they will be able to help her to buy an apartment when she is older.

In contrast, Paul Banda's family who live in Bulawayo in Zimbabwe have no savings. His parents have actually spent more than they have earned this year. They have had to borrow to cover the rent of their overcrowded apartment. Paul's father has a relatively low-paid job and his mother has recently lost her job. The family are concerned about how they are going to manage.

8.1 Apartment block in Hangzhou, China

The nature of saving

KEY TERM

Saving: disposable income that is not spent.

Saving in economics means not spending. Some people may keep their savings at home. Most put their savings into a financial institution such as a bank. A number of people save regularly while others save infrequently. Some people do not save at all.

When people save, they are postponing spending. If $20 is saved this week, it is not spent by the saver. The saver will, however, be likely to spend it in the future.

KEY TERMS

Disposable income: income after income tax has been deducted and any state benefits.

Dissaving: negative saving, spending more than disposable income.

Economists define saving as **disposable income** minus spending. Disposable income is income that people are free to decide what they do with it. It is the income they receive less income tax and plus any state benefits they receive. They can spend or save it.

It is possible for people to spend more than their disposable income, at least for a while. This is known as **dissaving**. If someone has a disposable income of $600 this week, they may be able to spend $800 if they use some of their past savings or they borrow or sell some of their assets.

INDIVIDUAL ACTIVITY 1

Using Table 8.1, calculate how much a person saves as their income rises.

Table 8.1

Disposable income per week ($)	Spending per week ($)
100	110
200	200
300	270
400	350
500	410

China's high saving ratio

KEY TERM

Savings ratio: the proportion of disposable income saved.

Chinese families, on average, often save as much as 25% of their disposable income. This is high compared to most countries. For instance, in 2017 Canadians saved 5% and Zimbabweans had a negative **savings ratio** of 6%.

There are thought to be a number of reasons why the Chinese save. One is that it is a tradition. The Chinese have got into the habit of saving. This is partly because in the past, it was not always easy for Chinese families to get loans from banks. This led to them saving in case of emergencies and to make large purchases. Housing remains expensive in the country and households often have to save up in order to put a down payment of as much as 30% of the price.

China is developing its welfare system, providing support for the unemployed and the old. The Chinese have been used to saving for old age and now that they are living longer, they are saving to add to their state pensions when they retire. They also save in case of illness. While there is some free healthcare in the country, people often have to pay for more complex medical treatments.

Why do people save?

People save for a number of reasons including:

- To purchase expensive items. For example, a family may save up to buy a car or a home.
- To provide a safety net. Families may have unexpected expenses. For example, a family may have to pay to have their home repaired after a storm.
- To take advantage of unexpected opportunities. For example, a family may be offered the chance to go on a foreign holiday at a reduced price.

- To spend on their children's education. In some countries, families have to pay to send their children to school, and in many countries university students have to pay tuition fees and to maintain themselves while they are studying.
- To spend on their healthcare. In some countries, people have to pay to receive medical treatment.
- To finance their retirement. The governments of some countries provide state pensions for those over a certain age. Even in these countries, most people have to save to ensure that their lifestyle is not too different from what they enjoyed when they were working.
- To make money. Saving can earn interest or, in Islamic countries, a share of profits.

GROUP ACTIVITY 1

Which of the following are reasons why people save?

a as a precaution
b as a way of increasing spending in the future
c to increase the quality of life when older
d to reduce wealth
e to spend on food.

Influences on how much people save

There are a number of influences on the amount people save. These include:

- Age. The amount people save can vary over their lifetime. When people just start working, they may not have enough income to save. When they are a little older, they may earn sufficient income to be able to save towards buying a home. They may also start to save for their children's education and their own retirement. In old age, people are likely to use rather than add to their savings.
- Confidence. If people are more confident about the future, they may save less. They may spend a relatively high proportion of their income now in the expectation that their disposable income will rise in the future. If they think their jobs are secure, they may also be less worried about coping with unexpected events.
- Culture. Some countries, such as China, have a history of people saving a relatively high percentage of their disposable income.
- Disposable income. When people are poor, they are likely to have to spend all of their disposable income just to buy basic necessities. They may not be able to save anything. As people's disposable income rises, they will be able to buy not only basic necessities but also some luxuries. They will also have some disposable income that they can save if they wish.
- Quality of banks. People are likely to save more if their country's banks provide them with a variety of reliable saving schemes.
- **Rate of interest** or share of profits. The rate of interest, or share of profits, is the reward for saving. The higher the rate of interest, or share of profits, the more people are likely to save. The rate of interest may, for example, be 5% per year. In this case, a person who saves $500 would receive $525 if they cashed in their savings at the end of the year. The rate of interest, as well as the reward for saving, is also the cost

KEY TERM

Rate of interest: a reward for saving and a charge for borrowing.

of borrowing. This is a connected reason why a higher rate of interest is likely to encourage saving. People will know that borrowing will be more expensive and so they will be more reluctant to borrow to meet unexpected expenses and to pay for expensive items.

- Tax treatment. Some governments encourage saving by not taxing the interest earned on saving or taxing it at a low rate.
- **Wealth**. The influence of wealth is rather uncertain. Wealthy people can afford to save. They may also be able to get a higher rate of interest per dollar saved if they save a large amount with a bank. Wealthy people, however, may think that they do not need to save much as they already have a financial safety net.

KEY TERM

Wealth: a stock of assets including money held in bank accounts, shares in companies, government bonds and property.

GROUP ACTIVITY 2

Decide whether the following would be likely to decrease or increase the amount people save:

a a fall in the price of food

b a fall in the rate of interest

c a rise in income tax

d a rise in the amount the government gives state pensioners

e expectation that more people will lose their jobs in the future

f the abolition of university tuition fees

g the opening of new banks.

The effects of saving

Saving provides people with a safety net to cope with declines in their incomes or with emergencies. This can help prevent them falling into poverty. It can also help them enjoy a reasonable standard of living when they retire.

Saving can also provide firms with the finance to expand. This will occur if the money saved is placed in banks and the banks lend the money to firms. The money may be used by firms to stay in business or expand. Firms expanding can benefit a country as more output can be purchased and it is likely that more jobs would be created.

There is a risk, however, that if an increase in saving is accompanied by a fall in spending, firms would be discouraged from expanding. Instead, they may reduce their output and make some of their workers redundant.

DISCUSSION POINT

What proportion of your disposable income do you think you will be able to save when you start working?

Summary

In this chapter you have learned that:

- Saving occurs when people do not spend all of their disposable income.
- The amount people save varies between individuals, families and countries.
- People can spend more than their disposable income if they use some of their savings, borrow or sell some of their assets. Chinese families save a relatively high proportion of their income because of habit, to purchase homes and to provide a safety net.
- People save to buy expensive items, to cover emergencies and unexpected opportunities, to pay for their children's education, to pay for healthcare, to finance retirement and to make money.
- People tend to save more as their disposable income rises.
- An increase in the rate of interest and a fall in confidence usually causes saving to rise.
- People's saving tends to vary over their lifetime with some dissaving occurring when they are older.
- Some governments try to encourage saving by providing tax incentives.
- Saving provides people with a safety net and money they can draw on when they retire.
- Saving can provide finance that firms can use to expand but if a rise in spending causes a fall in spending, firms may decide not to expand.

End-of-chapter questions

1 In what sense can saving be considered to be delayed spending?

2 Why may the Chinese save a lower proportion of their disposable income in the future?

3 How may a rise in the price of medical treatment affect savings?

4 Why may the rich save more than the poor?

5 Why are banks more likely to be willing to lend to the rich than the poor?

6 What effect will a fall in the rate of interest likely to have on borrowing?

7 If people become more optimistic about the future, what is likely to happen to saving?

8 What is likely to happen to saving at festival times?

9 When would a rise in saving not be accompanied by a fall in spending?

10 Will an increase in saving always benefit a country?

INDEPENDENT RESEARCH

Find out why Japanese household saving turned negative in 2014. See, for example, the article 'Japan's savings rate turns negative for first time', which you can search for on the *BBC News* website.

Firms closing factories and offices, and going out of business

In December 2016, Feye Mwangi lost his job when the tyre manufacturing factory he worked at in Nairobi, Kenya was closed down. Car firms in the country had one less source of tyres and shopkeepers near to the factory noticed a fall in their sales of, for instance, food and drink. The tyre factory was not the only factory to close down. In Kenya between 2011 and 2016, more than two million firms went out of business. Every year throughout the world, while new firms are set up, others stop producing. They sell off their buildings and equipment, and make their workers redundant. Workers like Feye Mwangi have to search for other jobs. Not all are successful in finding alternative employment.

9.1 A closed-down factory

Why do firms go out of business?

The main reason a firm goes out of business is because its costs are greater than its revenue. A firm may be able to borrow money to pay some of its costs for a while. It cannot, however, keep borrowing. It will run out of willing lenders as they will become worried that the firm will not be able to repay them. Other firms selling it raw materials and electricity, for instance, will also stop supplying if they are worried that the firm does not have the funds to pay.

A firm's costs of production

To produce a good or a service, a firm has to pay a number of costs. For example, car manufacturers have to pay their workers' wages, pay rent on their factories, pay for electricity, and pay for tyres, steel and other materials.

GROUP ACTIVITY 1

From the following list, identify **four** costs of producing wheat, **four** costs of providing train services and **four** costs of building houses.

a bricks
b fuel for tractors
c maintenance of track
d wages of carpenters
e wages of farm workers
f seed
g fertiliser
h ticket machines
i building plots
j carriages
k insurance
l roof tiles

Average total cost

KEY TERM

Average total cost: total cost divided by output.

Firms calculate the **average total cost** of producing their output. This is total cost divided by output.

$$\text{Average total cost} = \frac{\text{Total cost}}{\text{Output}}$$

It can also be called average cost. It is sometimes known as unit cost as it is the cost, on average, of producing one product. When a firm increases its output, its total cost will rise but its average total cost may fall if the firm becomes more efficient at producing the product. For instance, a higher output may enable a firm to make better use of its machinery. Buying a greater quantity of raw materials may also enable it to get a discount on its purchases. It is also possible that the average total cost will rise if production becomes less efficient. Table 9.1 shows a chair producer's total and average total cost.

Table 9.1 The total cost and average total cost of a chair producer

Number of chairs	Total cost ($)	Average total cost ($)
1	30	30
2	50	25
3	60	20
4	88	22
5	120	24
6	156	26

Cost curves

As well as drawing diagrams showing demand and supply curves, economists also draw diagrams showing cost curves. A firm's total cost curve will slope upwards from left to right as total cost rises with output. This is shown in Figure 9.1.

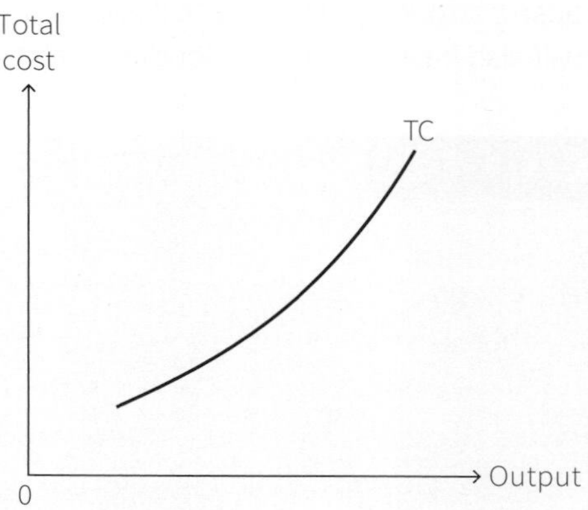

Fig. 9.1 A total cost curve

A firm's average total cost curve may be U-shaped, may slope down from left to right or may slope up from left to right.

INDIVIDUAL ACTIVITY 1

a Using Table 9.2 showing total cost, calculate a firm's average cost over the output shown.

Table 9.2

Output	Total cost ($)
1	100
2	180
3	240
4	280
5	300

b Plot the average total cost curve.

A firm's revenue

Revenue is the payment firms receive from selling their goods and services. If a firm sells ten bars of chocolate at $2 each, its total revenue will be:

$$10 \times \$2 = \$20$$

Its **average revenue** will be the same as the price it charges – $2, that is:

$$\frac{\$20}{10} = \$2$$

If a firm sells fewer bars of chocolate at the same price, its average revenue will be unchanged but its total revenue will fall.

KEY TERM

Average revenue: total revenue divided by the number of products sold.

The relationship between revenue and cost

KEY TERM

Interest: a payment made by a borrower to a lender of money.

If a firm's revenue is greater than its cost of production, it will make a profit. In contrast, if costs of production exceed its revenue, it will make a loss. In the short run, a firm may continue to produce if it is making a loss. It may borrow to finance some of its costs if it thinks that in the future, its revenue will rise or its costs will fall. It will have to be confident that its circumstances will improve. This is because borrowing will increase its costs. The firm will have to pay **interest** on its loans. It will also have to convince lenders that it will be able to repay.

INDIVIDUAL ACTIVITY 2

Calculate the following:

- **a** If a firm sells 2000 cars at a price of $9000 each, what is its total revenue?
- **b** It costs a firm $12 000 a week to make 60 beds. What is the average cost of making a bed?
- **c** A firm has earned a total revenue of $10 million and its total cost came to $7 million. What is its profit or loss?
- **d** A firm made a loss of $4 million. Its costs of production were $26 million. What was its total revenue?

GROUP ACTIVITY 2

In the early years of the twenty-first century, Delta Airlines was one of the most profitable airlines in the USA. In 2005, however, it ran into difficulties. It faced increased competition from new airlines and higher fuel costs. It nearly went out of business but managed to survive by cutting its labour costs and by introducing new routes.

- **a** What effect may greater competition have on a firm's revenue?
- **b** Explain **two** ways a firm could cut its labour costs.

GROUP ACTIVITY 3

Essar Steel India made losses between 2013 and 2017. The firm had borrowed large sums of money between 2007 and 2014 to expand its output. It had not expected the fall in demand for steel that started in 2015.

- **a** What do you think happened to steel prices in 2015 and why?
- **b** What would encourage a firm to expand its output?

DISCUSSION POINT

Does it matter if firms go out of business?

Summary

In this chapter you have learned that:

- When firms go out of business, their workers lose their jobs.
- Firms may go out of business when their costs are higher than their revenue.
- Costs of production include wages, rent, electricity bills and raw material costs.
- Average total cost is the cost per unit. It is total cost divided by output.
- Whether average total cost falls or rises with output will depend on whether the firm has become more efficient.
- Total cost rises with output.
- A total cost curve will slope up from left to right.
- An average total cost curve may be U-shaped, downward sloping or upward sloping.
- Average revenue is total revenue divided by the quantity sold. It is the same as price.
- Profit is made when revenue is greater than costs.
- When costs are greater than revenue, a loss is made.
- A firm may try to stay in business even if it is making a loss, if it thinks it will make a profit in the long run.

End-of-chapter questions

1 Why might unemployment not rise when one firm goes out of business?

2 What would explain a firm's profit rising when its costs increase?

3 Why may a firm make a loss one month and a profit the next month?

4 Identify **two** costs of operating an airline.

5 If 20 units are produced at a unit cost of $4, what is the total cost?

6 If a firm becomes less efficient, what will happen to the average total cost?

7 Why might a firm's average total cost be U-shaped?

8 What would cause a firm's total revenue to fall while its average revenue remains unchanged?

9 If a firm charges a price of $6, what is its average revenue?

10 If a firm makes a loss of $200 a day and its total revenue is $7500 a day, what is its total cost a day?

INDEPENDENT RESEARCH

Find out the reasons why Toys 'R' Us went out of business in 2018 and the possible consequences. See, for example, the articles entitled: 'Toys R Us and Maplin face collapse with 5,500 jobs at risk' (BBC Business News, 28 February 2018) and "Bosses knew something we didn't"' (BBC News Newsbeat, 28 February 2018) which can be searched for on the BBC News website.

Shopping options

Alberto de Soto lives in Peru's capital, Lima. His favourite subjects at school are economics and art. He enjoys reading and collecting books on these two subjects. Lima provides him with a wide variety of bookshops. Some are small, stocking a small number of books but often specialising in particular subjects. Alberto has got to know the owners of some of the small bookshops. They often put books to one side to show Alberto when he comes in.

Alberto also likes going to one of the large bookshops in the centre of Lima. He regularly has a cup of coffee in the coffee shop within the bookshop. He likes the variety of books the shop has and the exhibits it often puts on. He has also queued up at some of the book signings that the shop hosts.

10.1 A bookshop

Small firms

Some shoppers like buying from small firms. This may be because, like Alberto, they build up a friendly relationship with the owner. It is possible that the owner will be prepared to make adjustments to the product to suit the shoppers. The owner may get to know the requirements of their shoppers. For instance, some people like to buy their suits from a small tailor who knows them personally and can make them to measure. Indeed, many small firms have workers who make hand-made products, designed to meet the individual needs of their customers.

GROUP ACTIVITY 1

Which of the following do you think are used by economists to measure the size of firms?

a the number of hours it works in a year

b the quantity of products it produces

c the number of workers it employs

d the value of the products sold.

Large firms

If small firms often provide a personalised service, why do some shoppers prefer large firms? In some cases, they may not have any choice. The only firms producing the product, or that shoppers can buy from easily, may be large. For instance, in many countries, all the gas suppliers are large. In other cases, it may be because the shoppers think they will gain more from buying from large firms. What advantages do they think they may gain? The two key ones are lower prices and better quality. To consider whether shoppers are likely to benefit from buying from large firms, it is useful to first consider how and why firms grow in size.

The growth of firms

KEY TERMS

Merger: the joining of two firms to form one firm.

Market power: the ability of a firm to raise the price of its product without losing sales.

A firm that is popular with shoppers is likely to earn high profits. It may use some of these profits to expand production by building more factories, offices or shops and taking on more workers. This type of growth may take some time.

A quicker way for a firm to grow is to merge with another firm. A **merger** as a way of growing may also have the advantage for the firm that it may remove a competing firm. This will give the firm what economists call greater **market power**. With fewer rivals, the firm will have more ability to charge the price it wants to. If before it had decided to increase its price, some of its customers could have switched to its rival.

INDIVIDUAL ACTIVITY 1

Figure 10.1 shows the percentage shares of the UK grocery market in 2017.

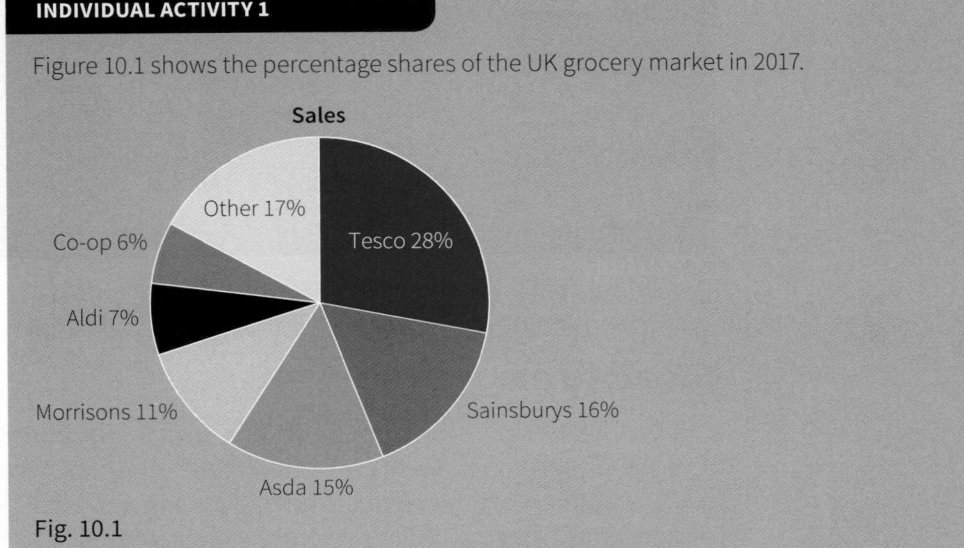

Fig. 10.1

a What percentage of sales are accounted for by the three largest supermarkets?

b Which supermarket is likely to have employed the most workers?

The benefits of firms getting larger

It is possible that shoppers will be able to enjoy lower prices and better quality as a result of firms getting larger.

Prices may be lower because average total cost may fall as a firm produces a larger output. There are a number of reasons for this. One is that a larger firm will buy more raw materials, equipment and services from other firms. Buying large quantities may enable a firm to negotiate discounts on the amount it pays its suppliers.

As a firm grows in size, it may be able to make use of large, efficient machines that can produce enough sales to make efficient use of such machines. For example, a machine that costs $500 a day to rent may be capable of producing 100 units of a good a day. If the price that can be gained per unit produced is $8, a small firm that only has demand for 20 units would make a loss of $340 ($160 revenue – $500 cost). In contrast, a large firm that can sell 100 units would make a profit of $300 ($800 – $500 cost).

KEY TERM

Economies of scale: the advantages of producing on a large scale.

A larger firm may be able to afford specialist workers who can help to lower its average total cost. For example, a large car firm may employ a team of car designers. These designers may come up with ideas that reduce production costs. They may also improve the quality of the cars produced.

Economists call the reasons why average total cost may fall when a firm increases its size, **economies of scale**.

GROUP ACTIVITY 2

Decide which may enable a growing firm to reduce its price:

a obtaining large loans at a lower rate of interest

b running training courses for 200 rather than 20 workers

c using large lorries to transport its product to retail shops.

The disadvantages of firms getting larger

There is the possibility that shoppers may experience higher prices and/or lower quality as a result of firms getting larger.

A large firm may be able to charge a lower price and offer a better quality product but may decide not to do so. A firm may get larger by merging with its competitor or driving its competitor out of business. In these cases, it may decide to raise the price it charges to get more profit. Its customers will either have to pay the price or go without the product.

The lack of competition a larger firm faces may also make it lazy. It may not spend time and effort trying to improve the product. Over time, the product may become out of date and less suited to customers' requirements.

It is also possible that as a firm gets larger, its average total cost may rise. This may occur if, for instance, the firm becomes more difficult to manage. There will be more activities to coordinate and more workers to communicate with.

DISCUSSION POINT

Do you think you would benefit from your school getting larger?

Summary

In this chapter you have learned that:

- Shoppers may like buying from small firms because of the personal service and individually made products they may provide.
- Firms may grow by building new production units or by merging. Large firms may be able to charge lower prices because they may have lower average total costs.
- Large firms may have lower average total costs because they can buy in bulk, use large machines efficiently and employ specialist workers.
- Large firms may be able to produce high-quality products because they can afford to spend more on research and development.
- Large firms may charge high prices and produce low-quality products because of lack of competition and because large firms may become more difficult to manage.

End-of-chapter questions

1. Why is a publisher of books on beetles likely to be smaller than a publisher of books on gardening?
2. Why do shoppers like low prices?
3. What effect is a rise in average total cost likely to have on prices?
4. Why may a firm get smaller in size?
5. Why are mining firms likely to be large?
6. How may improving the quality of products help a firm grow in size?
7. Why may a supplier of coffee be prepared to sell it for a lower price per unit to a large firm with coffee shops throughout the world than to a small firm with only three coffee shops?
8. Why may patients receive better treatment in large hospitals?
9. Why may a firm be considered to be large in its own country but small in global terms?
10. Will advances in technology improve communication between managers and workers?

INDEPENDENT RESEARCH

Take notes on why small firms are able to survive. Search for 'Study Notes: Small Businesses' in the 'Economics' section of the *tutor2u* website.

Also find out what is meant by diseconomies of scale. See 'Study Notes: Diseconomies of Scale' in the 'Business' section of the same website.

Chapter 11
Why does pollution occur?

Pollution in cities

In November 2017, the smog in Delhi, the capital city of India, was so bad that Prisha Arya had to cover her face when walking to school. One of her friends had to go to hospital because she had a serious asthma attack, brought on by the particles and toxic chemicals in the air. Breathing in the city's air was described as smoking 50 cigarettes a day. In that month Delhi became the most polluted city in the world. The city recorded an air quality index of 999 (the higher the number, the more pollution). The hazardous level starts at 300.

Flights to Delhi were cancelled, trains were either delayed or cancelled and there was an increase in car accidents because of the reduced visibility. There was a 20% increase in patients with pollution-related illnesses.

Among the cities with the highest levels of air pollution in 2017 were Onitsha, Kaduna and Aba in Nigeria; Peshawar in Pakistan; Gwalior, Allahabad and Delhi in India; and Riyadh and Al Jubail in Saudi Arabia.

11.1 School children wearing anti air pollution masks in New Delhi, India

The problems caused by pollution

There are a number of types of pollution. These include air pollution, noise pollution, water pollution, soil (land) pollution and visual pollution. Air pollution can cause a range of illnesses including lung cancer, strokes, and heart disease and respiratory infections. Noise pollution can harm people's hearing and make it difficult for them to sleep. Water pollution can also harm people's health – causing, for instance, diarrhoea – and damage to wildlife. Soil pollution reduces the natural fertility of farmland. Visual pollution occurs when people's ability to enjoy a view is reduced.

GROUP ACTIVITY 1

Decide what type of pollution the following actions would cause:

- **a** loud music
- **b** burning of coal
- **c** industrial waste deposited in rivers
- **d** people arguing loudly in the street
- **e** the release of carbon monoxide by factories
- **f** sewage dumped at sea
- **g** deforestation
- **h** the burial of nuclear waste
- **i** billboards hiding the view of a historic building
- **j** haze.

The causes of pollution

Some pollution is caused by natural disasters. Flooding and hurricanes can cause a range of waste and harmful substances to enter rivers, and desert storms reduce air quality. Most pollution is, however, caused by humans. People drive cars and fly on planes that cause noise and air pollution. Some farmers damage soil quality by overuse of pesticides. Water pollution is caused by the dumping of waste material into rivers and seas, fertilisers leaking into rivers and seas and by oil spillages. Some industries emit harmful gases, including sulphur dioxide and carbon monoxide from their factories.

Why do we create pollution?

Much of the pollution we create harms other people. If we had to pay for the harm we cause other people, or even if we were just more aware of the consequences of our actions, we might behave differently. For instance, a person in deciding whether to drive their car into a city centre at a busy time of the day is likely to only consider the costs to themselves. These will include the cost of petrol and the cost of parking. They are unlikely to consider the air pollution and the congestion they may contribute to. Sometimes we may have some awareness of the harm we will cause others, but we put our interests first. For instance, a firm may find it easier and cheaper to dump waste into a river than pay for it to be taken away and disposed of safely in a way that does not cause environmental damage.

KEY TERMS

Social cost: the total cost to society.

Private costs: costs borne by those directly consuming or producing a product.

External costs: costs imposed on those not directly involved in the consumption and production activities of others.

Social, private and external costs

Economists call the full costs of our activities, **social cost**. The social cost of people driving includes fuel costs, pollution, congestion and accidents. Economists divide social costs into:

- **private costs**
- **external costs**.

This division helps to explain why pollution occurs. Private costs are the costs paid by those who undertake the activities. In the case of driving, one private cost is the cost of petrol. External costs are the costs imposed on others such as pollution and congestion. Drivers impose costs on other motorists, pedestrians and people in their homes.

GROUP ACTIVITY 2

Decide whether the following are private or external costs of air travel:

a the wages of pilots

b the fuel for the planes

c traffic congestion near the airports

d a fall in the price of property near airports

e maintenance of the planes

f disturbance to the sleep of people living near the airport

g insurance of the planes.

KEY TERM

Third parties: those affected by the activities of others.

Third parties

Third parties are those who experience external costs and/or external benefits. The first and second parties to an economic transaction are the consumers and producers.

GROUP ACTIVITY 3

Identify three groups of people who may be considered to be third parties concerned with the building and operation of a new factory.

Economists and external costs

Economists can help reduce the problem of pollution and the other harmful effects that we impose on others. They can do this in three connected ways:

- identifying external costs
- measuring external costs
- suggesting ways of turning external into private costs.

Turning external costs into private costs

If we have to pay the full cost of what we consume and what we produce, we would have to think more carefully about our consumption and production decisions. We may, for instance, decide not to drive into a city centre at peak time if we know we will have to pay the full cost of this decision. If we do pay the full cost of our actions, the social cost will equal the private cost.

Economists have helped governments draw up policy measures to turn external costs into private costs. For instance, in many countries, governments fine firms that pollute. This moves the cost to the firms and encourages them to clean up their production process. A number of governments now impose a congestion charge on people who drive into city centres at busy times. Some local governments are also now considering allowing only electric cars to drive into their cities.

DISCUSSION POINT

What effect does tourism have on pollution?

GROUP ACTIVITY 4

Decide whether each of the following would be likely to reduce or increase the amount of litter in a city centre and why:

a the provision of more litter bins

b an increase in the fines for dropping litter

c the display of posters that explain the harmful effects of dropping litter

d a reduction in the frequency with which the city centre is cleaned.

DISCUSSION POINT

Will air travel cause more or less pollution in the future?

Summary

In this chapter you have learned that:

- Air pollution causes illnesses.
- The types of pollution include air pollution, noise pollution, water pollution, soil pollution and visual pollution.
- Pollution may be caused by natural disasters and human activities.
- Pollution is caused by people when they do not take into account the effect of their actions on others.
- Social cost is private costs plus external costs.
- Private costs are the costs experienced by those who undertake an activity.
- External costs are costs imposed on others.
- Pollution is an external cost.
- Economists can help reduce the problem of pollution by identifying and measuring the value of the external costs it causes and by suggesting ways to reduce it by turning external into private costs.
- Governments can fine those who cause pollution.
- Some governments impose a congestion charge on those who drive in city centres at busy times.

End-of-chapter questions

1 How may air pollution cause visual pollution?

2 Why is pollution an external cost?

3 Identify **two** ways farmers may cause pollution.

4 What would it mean if social costs equals private costs?

5 Are wages paid by a shirt manufacturer to its workers a private cost or an external cost?

6 Which type of costs do third parties experience?

7 Why may reducing private costs increase external costs?

8 Why may imposing taxes on firms that pollute reduce pollution?

9 What is the similarity between social cost and social benefit?

10 Identify **two** external costs that may be caused by people driving their cars into city centres at busy times.

INDEPENDENT RESEARCH

Find out about the causes and consequences of water pollution, for example, from the article 'Marine problems: Pollution', which you can find on the *WWF* website.

Will we run out of water?

Differences in the distribution and use of water

John Taylor lives in Bristol in the UK. He is often being told off by his parents for wasting water. He leaves the tap running when he is cleaning his teeth. He also likes having a shower in the morning and a bath in the evening after he has been playing football. In arguments with his parents, he has pointed out that he uses less water than they do. His parents regularly clean their cars and they use even more water filling the family's hot tub.

While John's family have some concern over the size of their water bill, Jamilah Osman and her family in Somalia are concerned about the lack of water. Jamilah and her family live in the village of Erdon. They have to walk four kilometres to a well to get water both for themselves and for the cows they keep. In 2017, after two years of no rain, Somalia experienced a drought. Two of Jamilah family's four cows died from lack of water and her young brother become seriously ill. Jamilah's brother did recover, but other people in the village died and some emigrated to Kenya.

12.1 Drought in Somalia

Water shortage

Many people cannot understand why the world has a shortage of water. They point out that water makes up 70% of the planet. What economists and environmentalists are referring to when they say that there is a shortage of water is that there is a shortage of clean, fresh water. It is this water that we drink, wash in, use in sanitation, give to livestock, use to irrigate agricultural land and use in manufacturing. This water is found in rivers, streams, lakes and underground. This type of water makes up only 3% of the world's supply of water and it is this water that is in short supply.

Nearly one billion people do not have access to enough water to keep them healthy. Even more, nearly two billion, experience shortages for at least one month a year.

Who uses water?

Households clearly use water, but their use accounts for less than 10% of the water consumed. Firms and farms also use water. Agriculture and food production account for more than two-thirds of all the freshwater used. It takes 100 litres of water to grow one kilogram of wheat and can take as much as 15 000 litres of water to produce one kilogram of red meat.

GROUP ACTIVITY 1

Match the following products from Table 12.1 with the number of litres of water it takes to produce them.

Table 12.1

Product	Number of litres
Almonds (1 kg)	1125
Car	2290
Litre bottle of a soft drink	3150
Pair of jeans	9450
Smartphone	14 400
T-shirt	81 000

Why does the water shortage matter?

Lack of clean fresh water to drink in, wash in and use in sewage systems leads to a variety of diseases including diarrhoea, typhoid fever and cholera. Diarrhoea alone causes more than two million deaths a year. Most of those who die are children.

There are also concerns that if the shortage increases, the disputes between countries over access to water may result in armed conflict.

Will the shortage of water get worse?

There is a risk that the water shortage will get worse. It is predicted that global water demand will rise by more than 20% between 2020 and 2050. There are a number of reasons for the expected rise in demand. One is the rising population. It is anticipated that world population will increase by 2.3 billion by 2050. Another reason is that incomes are likely to rise. As people get richer, they often eat more meat and buy more products that use up large quantities of water.

While demand is likely to increase, supply may decrease. It is possible that global warming may result in longer droughts. There may also be, at different times, more intense periods of rain. It is more difficult to collect water that comes down in heavy rainfall.

GROUP ACTIVITY 2

Which of the following do you think would increase demand for water?

a an increase in global tourism
b an increase in the number of households with toilets
c an increase in the number of people who drink tap water rather than soft drinks
d an increase in the number of people who are vegetarians.

KEY TERM

The economic problem: unlimited wants exceeding limited resources.

The economic problem

People wanting more water than there is water available illustrates what economists call **the economic problem**. This is the problem that there are not enough resources, such as workers and machines, to produce all the goods and services people would like to have. This is why choices have to be made.

What can governments do to reduce the shortage of water?

Economists suggest that if demand is greater than supply, either demand has to fall and/or supply has to increase. In some countries, there is a relatively high proportion of people who want more water but they cannot afford to buy it. In other countries, such as the UK, demand for water is high because the price is relatively low. It does not always cover the cost of treating and transporting the water. As water is under-priced in some countries, people waste it. It is not just households who waste it, suppliers also do. For instance, it has been estimated that more than 24 billion litres of water are lost each day in the USA from leaking pipes. If governments and firms were to spend more on upgrading treatment plants, water pipes and sewage systems, the shortage of water would be reduced.

Governments run campaigns encouraging people to save water. Some governments are going further. The Dutch government, for instance, taxes the use of tap water to encourage firms and households to use less water.

GROUP ACTIVITY 3

Decide whether the following would increase or decrease the global shortage of water:

a an increase in education about the global shortage of water
b a rise in the amount people eat
c a tax imposed on the use of water
d the replacement of old water pipes with new water pipes.

DISCUSSION POINT

Do you think the price of water should be increased in your country?

Summary

In this chapter you have learned that:

- Nearly a billion people lack sufficient access to clean fresh water.
- Water is used for many purposes including drinking, washing, sanitation, irrigating fields, giving to livestock and manufacturing.
- Agriculture is the main user of water.
- A lack of water reduces the quality of people's lives and causes a range of diseases.
- Demand for water is increasing.
- Water illustrates the economic problem; that is, what we would like to consume is greater than the resources we can produce.
- There are a number of measures a government can take to reduce the shortage of water. These include running campaigns to reduce the wastage of water, replace leaking water pipes and raise the price of water.

End-of-chapter questions

1 Is water evenly distributed among the world's population?

2 Do people overuse water?

3 What usually happens to price when demand exceeds supply?

4 What external benefits may be gained by ensuring everyone has sufficient access to water?

5 Until 2014, water was supplied free to Irish households. Why do you think the Irish government decided people would have to pay for water?

6 Will the economic problem ever be solved?

7 Why is demand for water increasing?

8 Why may a rise in the price of water result in a reduction in leakages from water pipes?

9 Why may a government be reluctant to tax water?

10 How does water pollution affect the problem of a shortage of water?

INDEPENDENT RESEARCH

Check out the progress that is being made towards ensuring that everyone has access to clean fresh water and sanitation, and the challenges being encountered, by visiting information on the United Nations' 6th sustainable development goal. Look for 'Ensure access to water and sanitation for all' on the *UN* website.

Smoking in China

Lui Ying does not like his father smoking. He does not like breathing in the smoke in the house he shares with his parents and he worries about his father's health. His father, Lui Chen, is one of the 350 million Chinese adults who smoke. Nearly half of all Chinese men smoke and China is the world's largest consumer and producer of cigarettes.

GROUP ACTIVITY 1

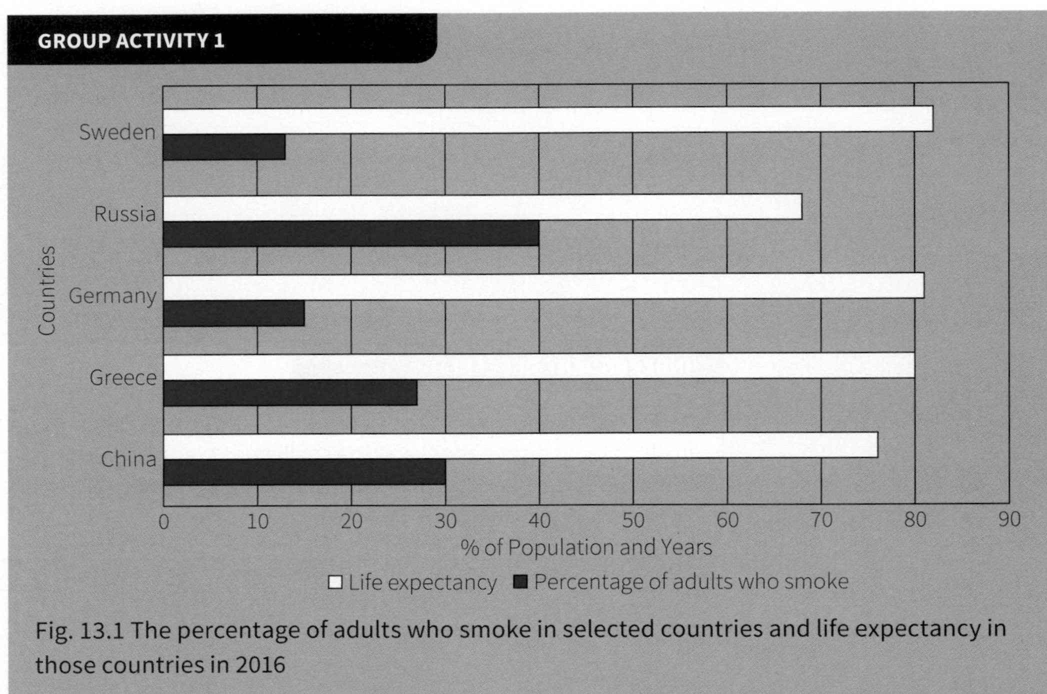

Fig. 13.1 The percentage of adults who smoke in selected countries and life expectancy in those countries in 2016

Using Figure 13.1:

a Explain whether the relationship between the proportion of adults who smoke and life expectancy is the one you would expect.

b Explain **one** other reason that may explain why life expectancy may vary between countries.

DISCUSSION POINT

Why do the rich smoke less than the poor?

Taxing cigarettes

Most governments tax cigarettes. One reason for this is to raise the price of cigarettes to reduce the number of cigarettes that people buy. Why does the government want to discourage smoking? It is for two reasons. One is that cigarettes harm the health of those who smoke. Some people who smoke get cancer, heart disease and other illnesses.

KEY TERM

Tax: a payment to the government.

The other reason governments tax cigarettes is because people smoking causes harm to other people. Non-smokers may breathe in the smoke coming from other people smoking. This can be unpleasant and may result in them suffering from the same illnesses as smokers. Non-smokers may have to pay higher **taxes** to provide the funds to provide medical treatment to smokers. They may also have to wait longer to be treated themselves because hospital beds are being taken up by smokers.

INDIVIDUAL ACTIVITY 1

Identify:

a a private cost arising from people smoking

b an external cost arising from people smoking.

Why do governments impose taxes?

Governments impose taxes for a number of reasons. One is to get revenue to spend on, for instance, education. Another is to discourage people from buying what economists call **demerit goods**. Cigarettes are an example of a demerit good. A demerit good has two characteristics. One is that the government thinks it is more harmful to those who buy it than they realise. The other is that it creates external costs.

KEY TERM

Demerit good: a product that is more harmful than people realise and that causes external costs.

GROUP ACTIVITY 2

Decide which of the following are demerit goods:

a education

b fruit

c guns

d high fat food.

How can a government reduce smoking?

As well as imposing taxes on cigarettes, governments use a number of other measures to reduce smoking. One is to provide information about the harmful effects of smoking. Healthcare campaigns may stop some people from smoking and may persuade other people not to start smoking. Another measure is to ban people under a certain age smoking. A government may also pass a law stopping people smoking in certain places. These may include restaurants, workplaces, cinemas, buses, trains and planes.

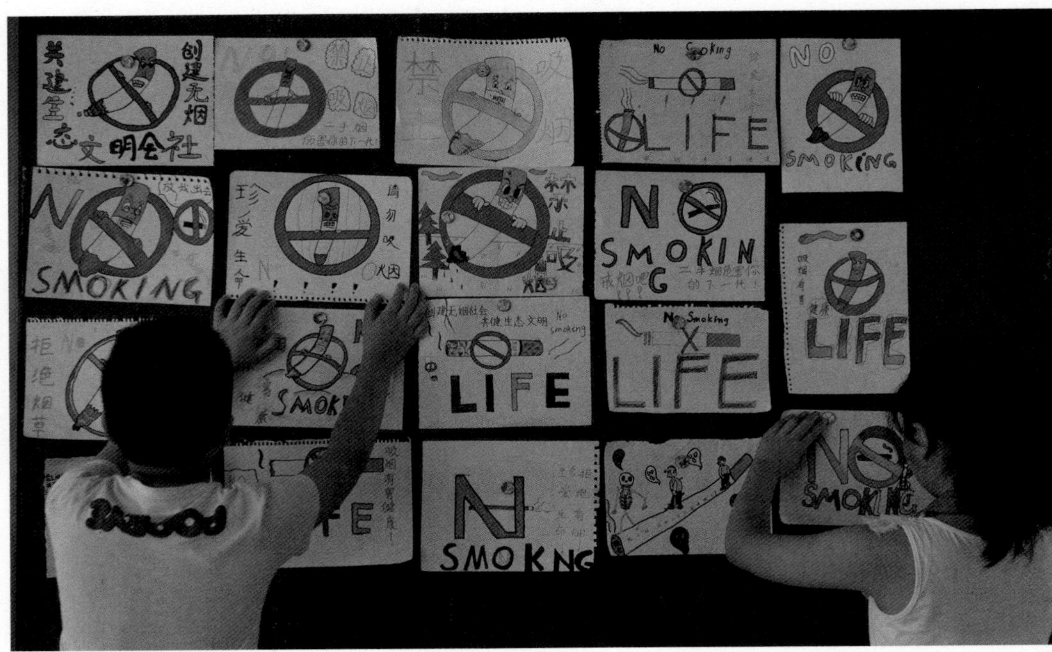

13.1 Students' posters drawn to discourage smoking

DISCUSSION POINT

Do you think governments should impose a complete ban on smoking cigarettes?

Summary

In this chapter you have learned that:

- The proportion of people who smoke varies between countries.
- Countries where a smaller proportion of adults smoke have a higher average life expectancy.
- Most governments impose a tax on cigarettes to discourage smoking.
- Cigarettes harm the health of those who smoke them and others who breathe in the smoke.
- Cigarettes are a demerit good.
- As well as discouraging the consumption of demerit goods, governments impose taxes to raise revenue.
- Demerit goods are more harmful than people realise and they impose external costs.
- Governments seek to discourage smoking by not only imposing taxes but also by running health campaigns, banning children smoking and banning smoking in public places.

End-of-chapter questions

1 What effect is a reduction in smoking likely to have on life expectancy?

2 Why may a tax on cigarettes discourage smoking?

3 Identify **two** private costs of smoking.

4 Identify a private benefit a person may gain from stopping smoking.

5 Why are cigarettes a demerit good?

6 How does a demerit good differ from a merit good?

7 What effect has a health campaign on smoking designed to have on demand for cigarettes?

8 A government reduces smoking by increasing a tax on cigarettes. How may this harm another objective of imposing a tax?

9 Why may banning smoking in public places reduce smoking?

10 Why are governments more likely to ban children than adults from smoking?

INDEPENDENT RESEARCH

Finland is intending to become the world's first smoking-free nation. Research how it is seeking to achieve this objective. For example, you could search for the article: 'How Finland could be a smoke-free country by 2030' on the *Cafébabel* website.

Chapter 14
What is money?

When money ceases to work

At the start of 2008, Esther Olonga's mother went to buy a loaf of bread in a market in Harare, the capital of Zimbabwe. The market trader asked for two billion Zimbabwean dollars. Mrs Olonga did not have this amount. She bargained with the shopkeeper who eventually accepted Mrs Olonga's scarf in exchange for the bread. By September 2008, prices were rising so rapidly in Zimbabwe that a loaf of bread could not be bought with the Z$ trillion bank note that had been issued by the country's central bank. Prices were no longer increasing by the amazing levels at the start of 2008, but were still making it difficult for Esther's family and other Zimbabwean families to buy the food and other items.

What is money?

Esther's family would like to have more money. Most of us would. This is because money lets us buy goods and services. Indeed, money is anything that can be used to pay for goods and services. For example, if a student sells his bicycle for $80, he can use the banknotes he receives to buy some books. He may also decide to save some of the money or use it to pay off a debt.

What items have been used as money?

You might be surprised to find out some of the items that have been used as money. They include seashells, leather strips, blankets, animal skins, grain, playing cards, gold and silver.

What is used as money today?

Banknotes and coins are still used in many countries, mainly to make small purchases. Together, banknotes and coins are sometimes called cash. Large purchases, and an increasing amount of small purchases, are being made by using money in bank accounts. This money is transferred in a variety of ways including using credit cards, debit cards and via the internet and smartphones.

How did money develop?

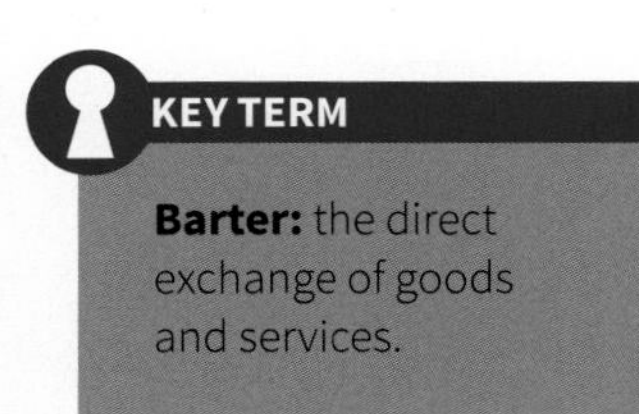

KEY TERM

Barter: the direct exchange of goods and services.

Before money, there was **barter**. This method is still used today when people lose confidence in money, such as occurred in Zimbabwe in 2008, and today with some internet transactions. Barter involves the direct exchange of goods and services, For instance, if a student wants to swap his bicycle for some books, he will try to find someone who has the books. There are, however, a number of problems with barter. One is that it may take time to find someone who is prepared to accept a bicycle for books. There may not be anyone who is willing to exchange books for a bicycle. Even if someone is found, it may be difficult to agree on a rate of exchange. For example, a person who has books the student wants may be willing to exchange only five books for the bicycle but the student may want eight books.

The direct swapping of goods and services may also involve a problem with giving change. The student may find someone who has four of the books he wants. He may not think they are worth the bicycle. It would not be possible for him to exchange half of his bicycle for four books.

Barter does not make it easy for people to save. The student may keep any books he receives for the bicycle but he cannot be certain how much he might be able to exchange his books for should he need to swap them in the future.

What does money do?

To act as money, an item has to be able to carry out four key functions:

- To buy and sell goods, and services. People use money to buy goods and services. Those who sell goods and services receive money in return. The sellers can then use the money they get to buy the products they want.
- To save. Money can be kept, usually in banks, to spend in the future.
- To compare values. We measure the price of goods and services in money. For instance, if your friend tells you that one pair of trainers is priced at $50 and another pair at $25, you will know that the first pair is twice as expensive as the second pair.
- To agree on how much has to be paid for borrowing money and how much will be received for lending money.

GROUP ACTIVITY 1

Decide which of the following you could do with money:

a lend it to someone
b save it in a bank
c spend it in a shop
d use it to measure the value of a house.

The characteristics of money

To carry out the functions of money, an item has to have a number of characteristics. These are to be:

- Generally acceptable. People have to be willing to accept the money as a means of payment.
- Easy to carry around. Taking a bicycle or books around shops in search of goods and services would not be convenient but it is easy to carry banknotes, coins and the means to transfer money from bank accounts.
- Durable. An item needs to last for some time.
- Available in different units. For example, there are $100, $20, $10, $5, $1 notes and various coins in the USA. This means that change can be given.
- Recognisable. People need to be able to identify the money of their country.
- Identical. Each dollar note is the same. This means that people do not place a greater value on one dollar note than another. They do not have to check the quality of the dollar note.
- Limited in supply. If everyone could get vast quantities of the item, people are unlikely to accept it as payment for goods and services. This is why, for instance, people living near a large forest, are unlikely to use leaves as money.

14.1 A customer hands money to a street vendor in exchange for goods

GROUP ACTIVITY 2

Explain **three** disadvantages of using eggs as money.

GROUP ACTIVITY 3

Research each of the multiple choice questions and then come to an agreed answer:

1 Which country uses the ringgit as its money?
   - **a** China
   - **b** Malaysia
   - **c** Singapore
   - **d** Thailand.

2 Which country is thought to be the first one to use paper money?
   - **a** China
   - **b** India
   - **c** Sweden
   - **d** USA.

3 Which country was the first to use ATMs (cashpoints)?
   - **a** France
   - **b** Germany
   - **c** UK
   - **d** USA.

4 Which item has not been used as money?
   - **a** cattle
   - **b** desks
   - **c** feathers
   - **d** soap.

DISCUSSION POINT

Do you think people will use coins and banknotes in the future?

Summary

In this chapter you have learned that:

- Money allows people to buy and sell products.
- Items that have been used as money include seashells, gold and silver.
- Current-day money includes banknotes, coins and money transferred between bank accounts.
- Money overcomes the need to barter.
- Barter requires people to have what other people want and be prepared to accept the products they want to swap.
- Barter makes it difficult to give change and to save.
- For an item to act as money it has to allow people not only to buy and sell products but also to save, to compare values, to borrow and to lend.
- The characteristics of money include general acceptability, easy to carry around, durable, available in different units, recognisable, identical and limited supply.

End-of-chapter questions

1. What is an opportunity cost of using gold as money?
2. Why do people accept money in exchange for goods and services?
3. Have postage stamps ever been used as money?
4. What items count as cash?
5. Why would bartering take time?
6. Why is it difficult to give change using barter?
7. What characteristic of money allows people to give change?
8. Why are durability and general acceptability important characteristics for money to have if people are going to save it?
9. What is meant by money being identical?
10. Why may someone in India not be prepared to accept an Australian banknote in exchange for a product?

INDEPENDENT RESEARCH

Find out more about the development of money by watching the video clip, 'A history of money in five objects' (BBC News Business, 'Money making: A brief history of currency from the British Museum', 22 April 2016) which you can search for on the *BBC* website.

Shopping in Venezuela in 2017

Prices in Venezuela in 2017 were not rising as rapidly as in Zimbabwe in 2007 and 2008 but they were increasing at an amazing rate. Between 2016 and 2017, the price of an average basket of goods and services increased by more than 2300%. Matais Salazar, who lives in Valencia in Venezuela with his parents, two brothers and sister, experienced some of the harmful effects of inflation. His parents earned 60 000 bolivars a month and most of this was spent on food. This was because food prices were so high. For instance, the price of a dozen eggs rose from 450 bolivars in 2016 to 1020 bolivars in 2017. Matais' parents got up early several days a week in 2017 to stand in long queues for hours to get money out of the ATM (cashpoint) and to make purchases in supermarkets. People were buying up food before it rose even higher in price and before it ran out. Indeed, Matais' parents often returned home without being able to buy the items they wanted because they had been sold out.

15.1 Empty supermarket shelves in Venezuela

KEY TERMS

Inflation: a rise in the price level of goods and services over time.

Price level: the average of current prices of goods and services in a country. Also sometimes called the general price level.

Inflation

Such a high rise in prices as recently experienced in Venezuela and Zimbabwe is not common. Prices do, however, usually increase over time. For instance, while some prices fell in Pakistan in 2017, the average rise in prices was 5.2%. Economists call a rise in a country's price level, **inflation**. The inflation rate is the percentage rise in the **price level** over time.

What causes prices to rise?

Firms increase the prices of their products for two main reasons. One is that they see a higher demand for their products. If people want to buy more products and are able to pay for them, firms can raise their prices and make more profits.

Prices may also rise because firms experience higher costs. If, for instance, wages rise or the price of the materials used to make products increases, firms may raise their prices to cover these higher costs.

GROUP ACTIVITY 1

Decide the **two** main reasons why a price level may fall.

Does a rise in prices matter?

KEY TERM

Purchasing power: the amount of goods and services that can be bought.

Goods and services may become more expensive but this does not always mean that people will not be able to buy as many of them as before. If people's income rises by more than prices, their ability to buy goods and services, called **purchasing power**, will increase. But some people's income may not increase by as much as prices. For example, the wages of farm workers may rise by 2%, while the price level may rise by 5%. If this is the case, farm workers will suffer. Other people may also suffer. Anyone who saves money and is paid a rate of interest below the inflation rate will have less purchasing power when her or his money is repaid.

Inflation can also make it difficult to make choices that will benefit people the most. For instance, a person may decide not to buy a car because it has risen in price by 4%. They may then find that other cars have risen by more than 4%. When they go back they may find that the car seller has now raised prices by 7%. The person will have missed out on the chance of a bargain because inflation has made it difficult for them to compare prices.

Very high rates of inflation can cause people to panic. As in Venezuela, they may rush to buy food before it goes up in price even more and shops may run out of food.

If a country's prices are rising by more than other countries' prices, the country's firms may find it difficult to sell their products at home and abroad.

GROUP ACTIVITY 2

Table 15.1 shows the inflation rate and the percentage increase in average wages in selected countries in 2017.

Table 15.1

Country	Inflation rate (%)	Increase in average wages (%)
Argentina	27.0	27.0
Egypt	24.0	5.2
Indonesia	3.8	4.3
South Africa	5.3	6.1
Turkey	11.1	7.2

Using the information in Table 15.1:

a In which country did the price level rise the most?

b In which countries would workers have been able to buy more goods and services in 2017 than in 2016?

Can a government control inflation?

Governments try to stop prices rising at too high a percentage. If they think that the inflation is caused by people spending too much, they will try to reduce the growth of spending. They may do this by increasing taxes and raising the rate of interest. If they think that prices are being pushed up by higher costs, they may try to reduce the growth of costs. They might, for instance, pay to train workers. If workers are more skilled, their output may rise, which may keep average costs down.

GROUP ACTIVITY 3

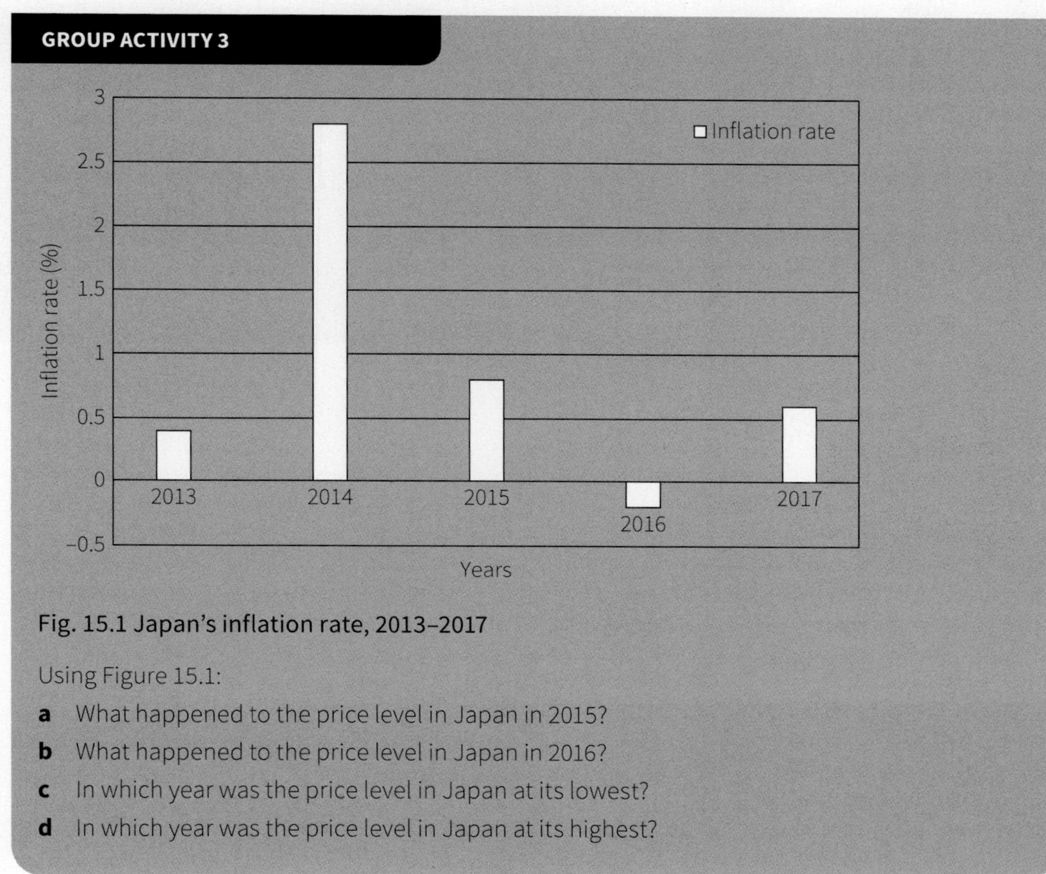

Fig. 15.1 Japan's inflation rate, 2013–2017

Using Figure 15.1:

a What happened to the price level in Japan in 2015?

b What happened to the price level in Japan in 2016?

c In which year was the price level in Japan at its lowest?

d In which year was the price level in Japan at its highest?

DISCUSSION POINT

Is inflation a problem in your country?

Summary

In this chapter you have learned that:

- When prices are rising rapidly and by large amounts, people have to spend longer shopping.
- The two main causes of inflation are higher demand for the country's goods and services, and higher costs of production.
- If people's income rises by more than prices, their purchasing power increases.
- Inflation can make it difficult to make choices as it may make it hard to determine which are the cheapest products.
- When the inflation rate is high and rising, people may try to buy products before their price rises even higher.
- If prices are rising by more than other countries, the country's firms may find it difficult to sell their products at home and abroad.
- Governments try to prevent prices rising too much.
- Among the measures that a government may take to reduce inflation are increasing taxes, raising the rate of interest and training workers.

End-of-chapter questions

1 What does an inflation rate of 6% mean?

2 Do all prices rise during inflation?

3 What are the **two** main reasons why people's purchasing power decreases?

4 Why may the poor suffer more from inflation than the rich?

5 Why may firms raise their prices when demand increases?

6 Why may increases in wages may cause inflation?

7 If people expect a higher rate of inflation, why may this cause prices to rise even further?

8 Why may inflation cause people to buy more products abroad?

9 If a country is experiencing inflation, why does a government need to know its cause?

10 Why may training workers reduce inflation?

INDEPENDENT RESEARCH

Find out who are the potential winners and losers from inflation and the reasons why. See, for example, 'Study Notes: Inflation – Consequences of Inflation' on the *tutor2u* website.

Why do some people leave Mexico to live in the USA?

Migration

In 2012, Juana Ramirez and her family left their home in Guadalajara in Mexico to live in Houston in the USA. Her father originally got a job as a taxi driver and her mother was employed as a housekeeper. Her father now has a job as a car salesman and her mother is employed as a nurse, a job she did in Mexico. Juana's older sister is setting up her own recruitment firm after graduating in communication studies from the University of Texas at Austin. Juana is hoping to study medicine and become a doctor when she leaves school in 2019.

16.1 Houston, Texas

Many people like to live close to where they grew up. This is because they are likely to have friends and family ties. Some people move away because they like adventure. But the main reason why people move to another country is to improve their living standards. This is why the Ramirez family moved. The parents thought that they would be able to provide their children with a better quality of life and a better future.

People born in Mexico make up the highest percentage of **immigrants** living in the USA. Since 2013, however, people from India and from China have accounted for a larger percentage of people entering the USA to settle. In 2015, for instance, 180 000 people moved to the USA from India, 145 000 moved from China and 140 000 from Mexico.

KEY TERMS

Migration: the movement of people from one place to another.

Immigrants: people coming from abroad to live in the country.

GROUP ACTIVITY 1

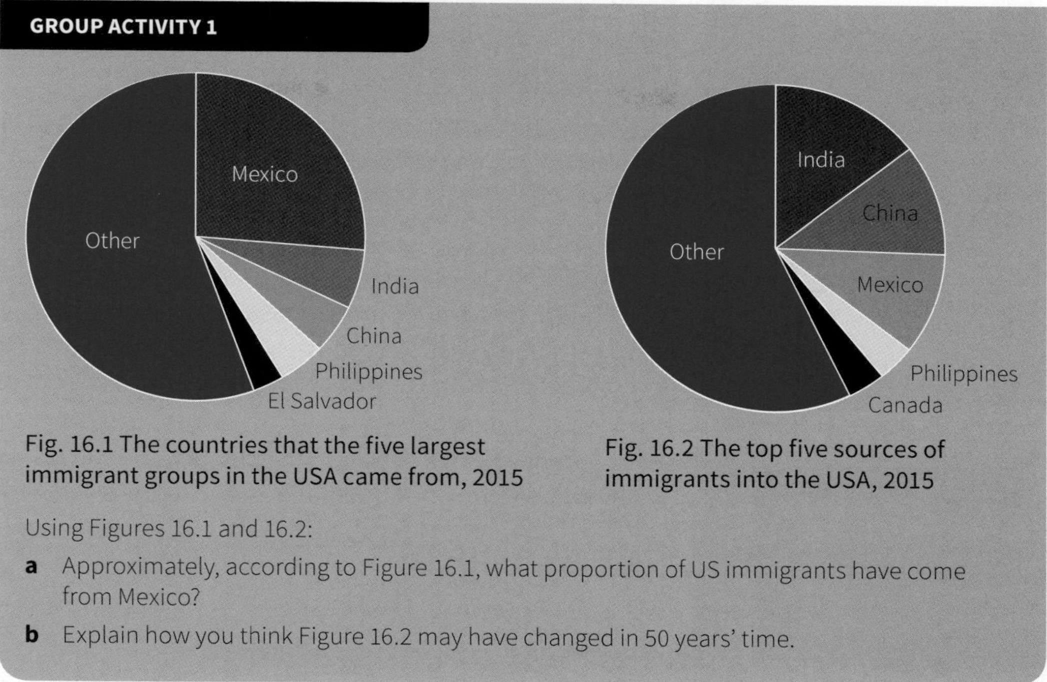

Fig. 16.1 The countries that the five largest immigrant groups in the USA came from, 2015

Fig. 16.2 The top five sources of immigrants into the USA, 2015

Using Figures 16.1 and 16.2:

a Approximately, according to Figure 16.1, what proportion of US immigrants have come from Mexico?

b Explain how you think Figure 16.2 may have changed in 50 years' time.

Reasons why people migrate

Surveys have shown that half of Mexicans believe that life is better in the USA and more than a third of Mexicans have said they would like to move to the USA. Geographers and economists sometimes refer to 'push' and 'pull' factors when they are examining the reasons why people migrate. Push factors are those that force people to leave their country, for example, religious persecution and famine. Pull factors are features of a country that attract people to move there.

GROUP ACTIVITY 2

Decide whether the following are push or pull factors causing people to migrate from Mexico to the USA:

a better quality of housing in the USA

b higher crime rates in some areas of Mexico

c shorter working hours in the USA

d the presence of family members in the USA.

DISCUSSION POINT

Would you like to live in another country?

Reasons why people migrate from Mexico to the USA

Mexicans are attracted to live in the USA because they think they will have better lives there. Among the things that they think will be better in the USA are:

- Better employment opportunities. Some people in Mexico may not be able to get a job. Some may be unemployed and so they move to the USA in search of a job. Others may believe that they may be able to get a job that will give them more satisfaction.

- Higher wages. On average, wages are higher in the USA than in Mexico. If people can get a better paid job, they can afford to buy more goods and services. They may, for instance, have a better house and may be able to buy a car.
- Better working conditions. Some Mexicans may be able to find a job in the USA in cleaner, and safer, offices and factories.
- Better education. Some Mexican parents may think that schools in the USA are better than those in Mexico. Going to a better school may increase their children's chances of gaining an interesting and well-paid job.
- Better healthcare. Mexico and the USA have a mixture of government-provided healthcare, free to patients, and healthcare that has to be paid for. Spending by the government on healthcare is now increasing in Mexico but it is lower than in many countries, including the USA.

KEY TERM

Birth rate: number of births per thousand of the population in a year.

There has recently been a decline in the number of Mexican immigrants. This has been caused by reduced job opportunities in the USA, improved job opportunities in Mexico, a long-term decline in the Mexican **birth rate** and tighter controls on the movement of people from Mexico into the USA.

The effects of emigration

What effect does the departure of some of its people have on Mexico? If people who leave were out of work, the country may benefit. This is because the country's government will have to spend less supporting the unemployed. But if those who emigrate were workers with important skills, the country will lose out. Firms may not be able to produce high-quality products and may take longer to produce products. There will also be fewer people in the country to buy goods and services so firms will produce less.

The effects of immigration

KEY TERM

Emigration: people leaving a country to live in other countries.

While **emigration** reduces the size of a country's population, immigration can increase it. Having more people may benefit a country. If the immigrants get jobs, the country's output will increase. Some immigrants may bring in skills that are in high demand or may be prepared to do jobs that workers born in the country are not willing to do. Immigrants also start new businesses.

There is also a risk that immigration may bring some disadvantages, at least in the short term. There may be pressure on housing, healthcare and schooling. Some immigrants may not find jobs and so may have to rely on the government for financial support.

INDIVIDUAL ACTIVITY 1

Six per cent of the US population of 325 million were born in India.

a Calculate the number of people living in the USA who were born in India.

b Explain **two** reasons why fewer people may move from India to the USA in the future.

DISCUSSION POINT

Would an economy benefit from a reduction in immigration?

Summary

In this chapter you have learned that:

- Some people move from one country to another to increase their living standards.
- Mexico has until recently been the main source of people moving to the USA. Now more people are coming from India and China.
- Push factors encourage people to leave their country while pull factors attract them to another country.
- People move from Mexico to the USA in search of better employment opportunities, higher wages, better working conditions, better education and better healthcare.
- Emigration may reduce unemployment in the country people leave. It may, however, result in a reduction in skilled workers and the country's ability to produce goods and services.
- Immigration will increase the size of a country's population.
- Among the benefits that may be gained from immigration are more skilled workers, new businesses being set up and higher output.
- Among the challenges that immigration may create are the need to find more housing, education and healthcare for the immigrants.

End-of-chapter questions

1 What is the difference between immigrants and tourists entering a country?

2 If higher wages in the USA is a pull factor for Mexicans, what is the corresponding push factor?

3 What effect has a fall in unemployment in Mexico likely to have on emigration from Mexico?

4 Do all Mexican immigrants enjoy a higher living standard in the USA?

5 Identify **two** influences on where in the USA Mexican immigrants may move to.

6 Do countries experience both emigration and immigration?

7 What effect will emigration have on the size of population of the country the people leave?

8 What effect may emigration have on the productivity in the country the people leave?

9 What effect may an increase in the quality of education in Mexico have on emigration of Mexicans to the USA?

10 Why may more Mexicans emigrate to countries other than the USA in the future?

INDEPENDENT RESEARCH

Research how migration affects India and why India has been described as a 'migration superpower'. See, for example, 'India is a migration superpower. Here's why' on the *World Economic Forum* website.

Chapter 17
Does it matter that the Japanese are getting older?

Different generations

Kenzou Iwata lives in Japan's capital, Tokyo. After he finishes school, the 15-year-old goes to a private tutor for an hour to get help with mathematics. He then visits his great-grandmother, Hisa Kato. She is aged 90 and lives in a nursing home. Kenzou helps his great-grandmother in a number of ways, including assisting her to move from her chair to her bed. A care assistant used to do this but the nursing home is now short of staff. The manager of the nursing home has told Kenzou's parents that, within the next few years, he is hoping to be able to use robots to help with the residents' care. Meijo University in Nagoya is developing a carer robot, called Robear, to carry out a range of functions including lifting patients out of bed and into chairs and wheelchairs.

Hisa Kato is visited not only by her great-grandson but also by her friends, Aiko and Banri Tonegawa who live in an apartment three streets away. They are younger than Hisa, at 84 and 83. Although they have one child, they do not have any grandchildren or great-grandchildren. They are worried who will look after them should they become infirm. They do not have much savings and there are waiting lists for state-run nursing homes.

17.1 Elderly residents in a nursing home in Japan

Japan's ageing and shrinking population

Japan's population is getting older and it is shrinking. The average age of its population is rising. It was 47 years in 2018, making it, with Germany, the world's oldest population. The global average was 31 in 2018.

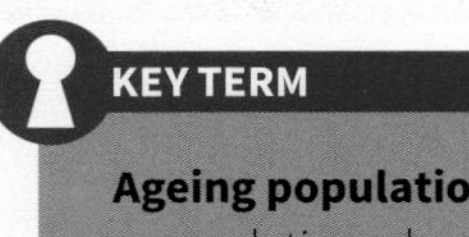

KEY TERM

Ageing population: a population whose average age is increasing.

Japan has the largest proportion in the world of over 65s in its population. In 2018, 26% of its population was aged over 65, compared with a global average of 8.5%. By 2050, it is predicted that 39% of the Japanese population and 17% of the global population will be aged over 65. Japan's population is also declining. It peaked at 128.6 million in 2005. By 2018, it had fallen to 127.2 million. It is predicted that it will fall to 92 million by 2050 and 50 million by 2120. If the current trend were to continue, it is possible there will be only one Japanese person by 3050!

INDIVIDUAL ACTIVITY 1

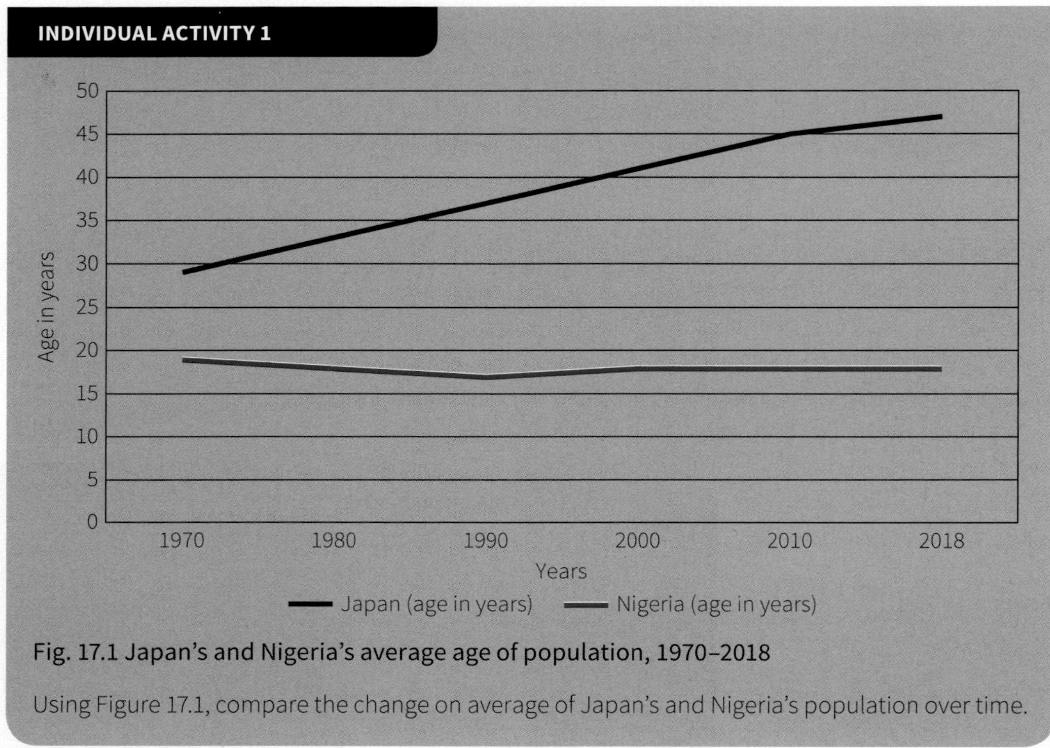

Fig. 17.1 Japan's and Nigeria's average age of population, 1970–2018

Using Figure 17.1, compare the change on average of Japan's and Nigeria's population over time.

Population pyramids

KEY TERM

Population pyramid: a diagram showing the age and gender structure of a country's population.

Economists and demographers (people who study population) make use of **population pyramids**. These are diagrams that show countries' populations in terms of the number of people of different ages. They also show the numbers of a country's population in different five-year age groups divided into males and females.

There are three main different shapes of population pyramids:

- expansive
- constrictive
- stationary.

Expansive shape

This has a smaller number of people in each age group as the ages rise. The countries that have such a population pyramid have relatively large numbers at a young age and a low life expectancy. Figure 17.2 shows an example of such a shape.

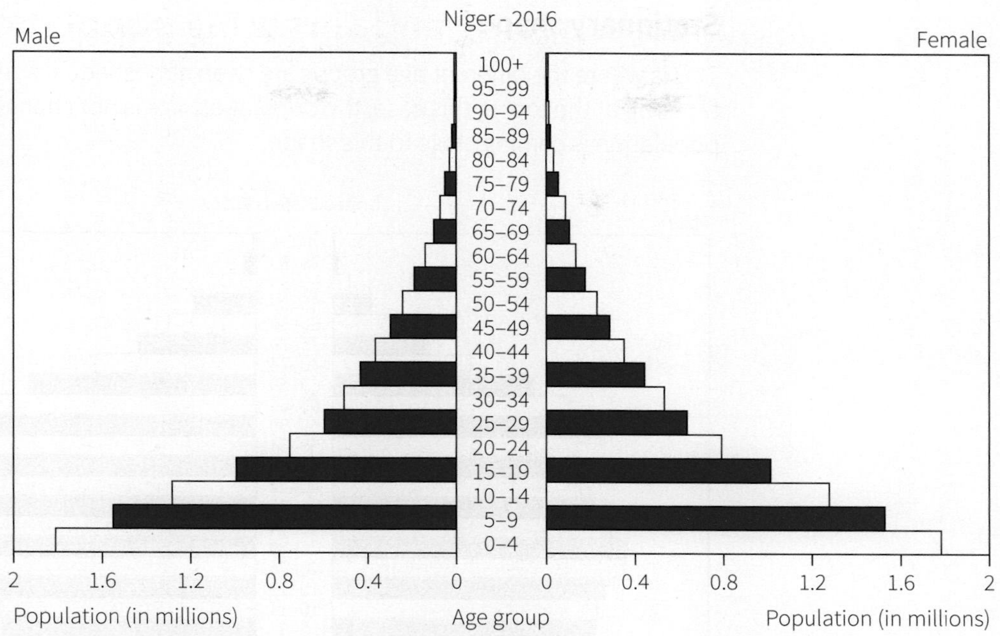

Source: Central Intelligence Agency (2018) *The World Factbook: Niger*, www.cia.gov/index

Fig. 17.2 Population pyramid of Niger, 2016. It has an expansive shape

Constrictive shape

A constrictive population pyramid occurs in the case of an ageing and shrinking population pyramid such as Japan. It has lower numbers at a younger age and tapers at the very highest ages and is sometimes said to look like the shape of a beehive.

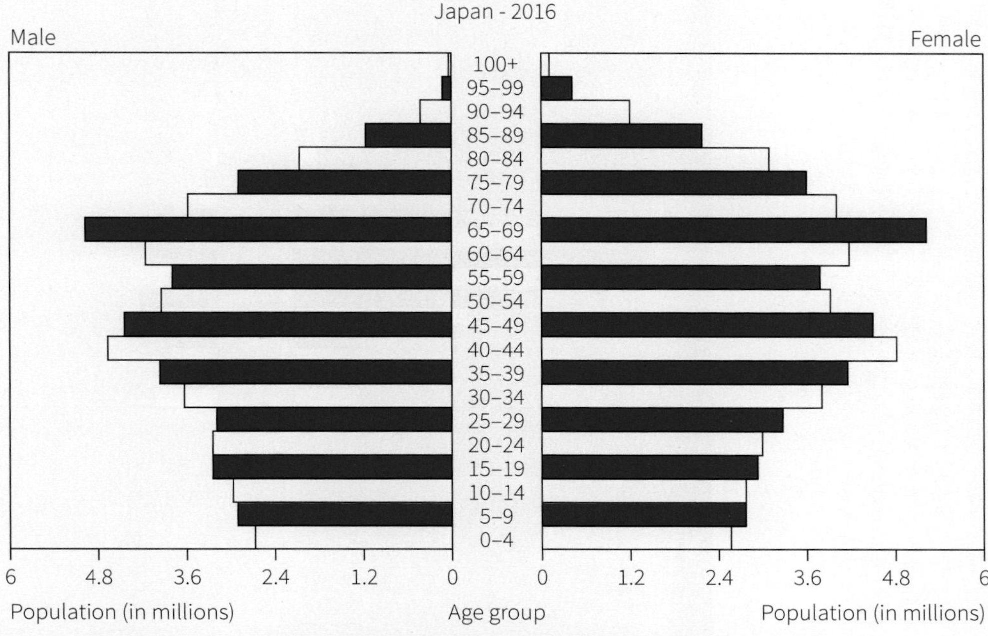

Source: Central Intelligence Agency (2018) *The World Factbook: Japan*, www.cia.gov/index

Fig. 17.3 Population pyramid of Japan, 2016. It has a constrictive shape

Stationary shape

This is where the different age groups are of an almost equal size, although with some tapering at the top. In this case, the population size is not changing much. The USA's population is coming close to this shape.

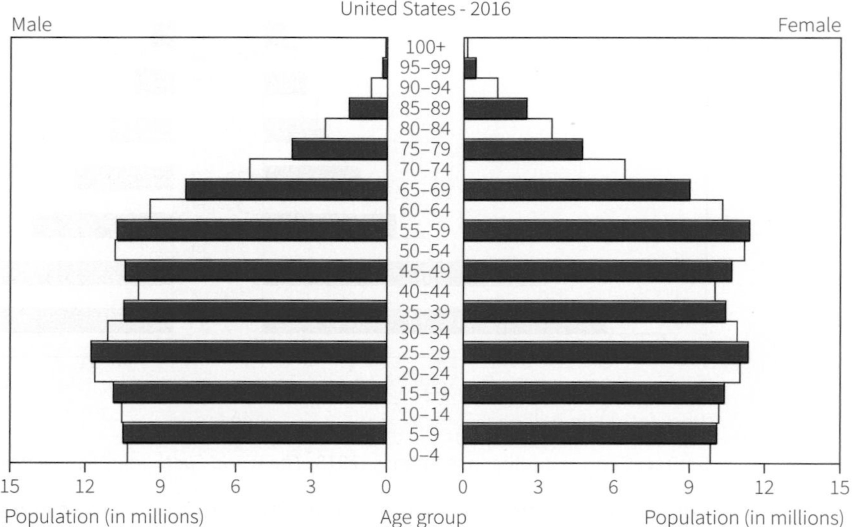

Source: Central Intelligence Agency (2018) *The World Factbook: USA*, www.cia.gov/index

Fig. 17.4 Population pyramid of the USA, 2016. It has a stationary shape

GROUP ACTIVITY 1

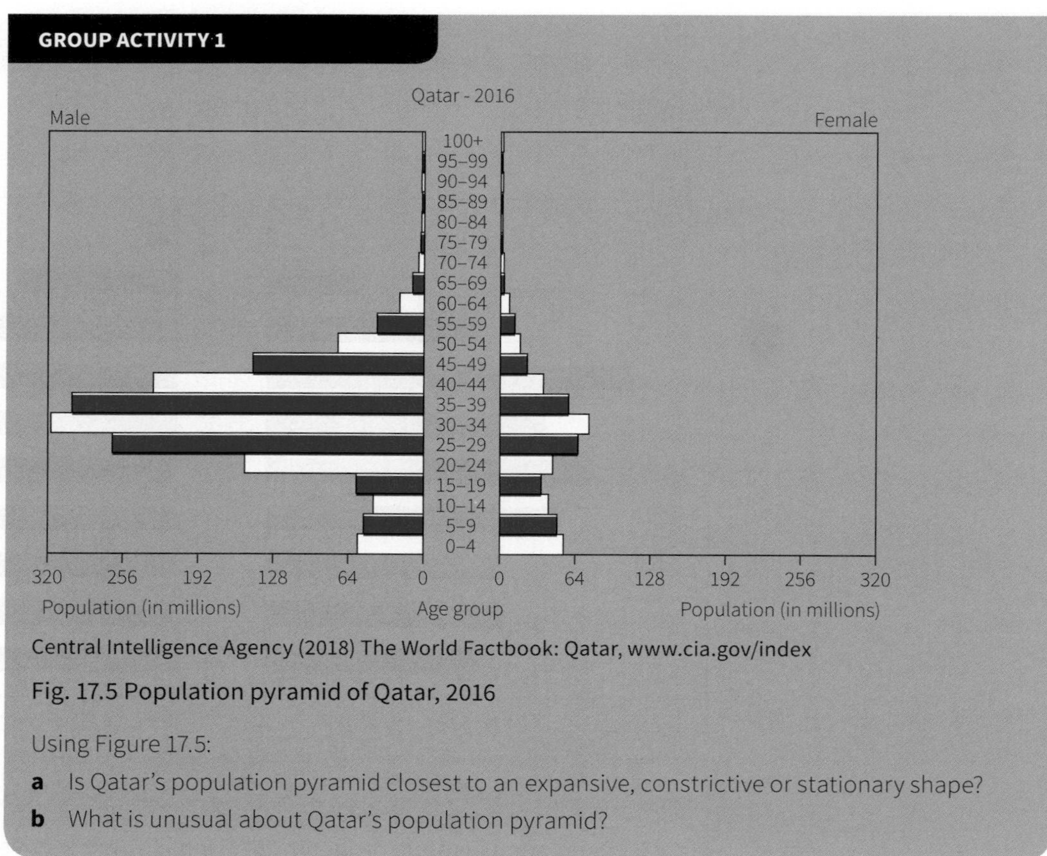

Central Intelligence Agency (2018) The World Factbook: Qatar, www.cia.gov/index

Fig. 17.5 Population pyramid of Qatar, 2016

Using Figure 17.5:

a Is Qatar's population pyramid closest to an expansive, constrictive or stationary shape?

b What is unusual about Qatar's population pyramid?

Causes of the changes in Japan's population

Why is Japan's population ageing and declining? It is because it has had, for some time, increasing life expectancy and a falling **birth rate**. Japan has one of the world's longest life expectancies. By 2018, it was 85 years. The Japanese have a high income, eat a healthy diet and they have been benefiting from improved healthcare.

KEY TERMS

Birth rate: number of live births per thousand of the population in a year.

Death rate: number of deaths per thousand of the population in a year.

While there is a high proportion of elderly people in Japan, there is a smaller proportion of young people. Both Japan's death rate and its birth rate are falling. Its birth rate is now below its **death rate**. The number of babies being born is not replacing the number of people who are dying. There are a number of reasons why Japan's birth rate is falling. These include the increased cost of raising children and couples delaying having children to follow their careers.

In some countries, a low death rate and low birth rate are offset by immigration. More people coming to live in the country may mean that its population size is still rising. Japan has, however, had very low immigration.

GROUP ACTIVITY 2

Decide whether the following are likely to increase the size of a country's population:

a an improvement in housing

b an increase in the quality of healthcare

c an increase in the proportion of the population who smoke

d a rise in the school leaving age.

The consequences of an ageing and declining population

There are a number of possible consequences of an ageing and declining population. These include:

- A fall in the size of the labour force. This may reduce the amount of goods and services the country is capable of producing.
- A greater burden being placed on workers. More taxes may have to be paid to support those who are retired. In 2018, there was 2.1 Japanese workers for every Japanese person over the age of 65. This is predicted to fall to 1 by 2070. Economists and demographers talk about an increasing **dependency ratio**.

KEY TERM

Dependency ratio: the proportion of the population that has to be supported by the labour force.

- A rise in the relative cost of healthcare. The elderly tend to place a greater burden on health services. For instance, it is predicted that by 2025, more than one in five elderly Japanese will have dementia.
- A rise in the cost of state pensions. If the retirement age is not increased, there will be more people who the government is paying a pension to.
- Waste of schools and other facilities. Some Japanese primary schools are only a quarter full.

DISCUSSION POINT

What may be the costs and benefits of a population getting younger?

Ways of reacting to an ageing and declining population

There are a number of ways a government may try to cope with an ageing and declining population and to try to reverse the changes. These may include:

- Automating more jobs. Greater use of machinery, including robots, may allow a smaller population to produce more goods and services.
- Encouraging an increase in the birth rate. It may attempt to do this by, for instance, reducing the cost of childcare and increasing child benefits.
- Encouraging immigration. If more people can be encouraged to come to live and work in the country, its dependency ratio may fall.
- Encouraging more people to take out private pensions. This would make it easier for a government to pay less in state pensions.
- Making it easier for people to work to a later age. This might be achieved by, for instance, increasing the proportion of part-time government jobs and allowing more government workers to work from home.
- Raising the retirement age. This would increase the proportion of workers to retired people, increase tax revenue and reduce the cost of pensions.

GROUP ACTIVITY 3

Decide which of the following would make it easier for a government to cope with an ageing population:

a an increase in income tax revenues

b a reduction in the amount of state pension paid

c net emigration of people of working age

d people working past retirement age.

Summary

In this chapter you have learned that:

- The average age of the Japanese is rising and its population size is declining.
- Population pyramids show the age and gender structure of a country's population.
- There are three main types of population pyramid – expansive, constrictive and stationary.
- Japan has a constrictive population pyramid.
- Japan's population is ageing and declining because the Japanese are living longer and having fewer children.
- The Japanese have a high life expectancy because they have a high income, eat a good diet and have good healthcare.
- The Japanese birth rate is low and declining because of the high cost of raising children and couples delaying having children.
- An ageing and declining population reduces the size of the labour force, places a greater burden on workers, increases the relative cost of healthcare and state pensions, and wastes some facilities.
- Governments may try to cope with an ageing and declining population by automating more jobs, encouraging an increase in the birth rate, encouraging immigration, encouraging more people to take out private pensions, making it easier for people to work at a later age and raising the retirement age.

End-of-chapter questions

1 Why might an ageing population be seen as a good thing?

2 What is the shape of a stationary population pyramid?

3 Why do population pyramids taper at the top?

4 Why do you think more educated women have fewer children than less educated women?

5 It is sometimes said that Japan is facing a demographic 'time bomb'. What do you think this means?

6 Identify **two** causes of a country's population getting younger.

7 Why may a cut in state pensions increase the birth rate?

8 What effect will a declining population have on a country's firms' ability to take advantage of economies of scale?

9 What effect will raising the retirement age have on government tax revenue?

10 Why might a rise in the retirement age in a country such as Japan be seen as fair?

INDEPENDENT RESEARCH

Compare the UK's and Mozambique's population pyramids. See, for example, 'Population structure and population pyramids', which you can search for on the BBC GCSE Bitesize website.

Chap
Why

Youth unemployment in Mauritania

Yann Ould Daddah lives in Nouakchott, the capital of Mauritania, a large West African country. He left school in 2016 and is still looking for a job. He has applied for 32 jobs but has yet to get an interview. His job prospects are not helped by his lack of qualifications and the difficulty he has with reading and writing. Nearly a third of 15–24-year-olds were unemployed in Mauritania in 2017.

Yann's parents are hoping that his brother, Achille, will find it easier to get a job. Achille is doing well at the newly built technical school. Achille would like to get a job as a geologist in the country's uranium mining industry. His job prospects will be influenced not only by his qualifications but also by how well the industry is doing.

Who are the people without jobs?

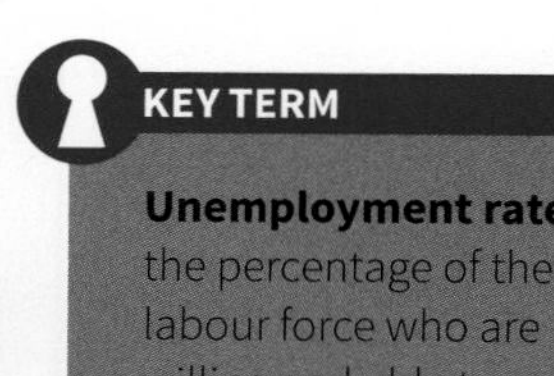

KEY TERM

Unemployment rate: the percentage of the labour force who are willing and able to work but are without jobs.

Children who are attending school and people who are retired do not have jobs. Some people who are of working age also do not have jobs. A number of these are not looking for work. They are, for instance, homemakers, in education or have retired early. Other people of working age are without a job and they want one.

The unemployed

An unemployed person is not just someone without a job. To be considered unemployed, a person has to be not only without a job but also to be willing and able to work. Governments calculate the number of people unemployed and the **unemployment rate**.

18.1 Unemployed people reading details about job vacancies

GROUP ACTIVITY 1

Decide which groups an economist would class as unemployed:

a people who are in the army

b people aged over 30 who are studying at university

c people who are devoting their time to bringing up their children

d people who have left university and are actively searching for employment

e people who have been sacked from their jobs and cannot find new jobs.

Causes of unemployment

There are a number of reasons why people who are actively seeking employment are without a job. These include:

- They may lack the right skills. There may, for instance, be people who have skills in farm work but the job vacancies may require IT skills.
- Jobs may be in different parts of the country. People may not be able to move to where the jobs are because they cannot afford the price of housing or because their family does not want to move.
- Some people may be between jobs. They may have left one job and be taking some time looking for another job.
- Some jobs are seasonal. They provide work only at certain times of the year. For example, fruit pickers may only be employed at certain times of the year.
- There may not be enough vacancies for the unemployed. If people in the country are not demanding many goods and services, there will be a shortage of jobs available.

KEY TERM

Labour force: people in work and those actively seeking work. It consists of the employed and unemployed.

INDIVIDUAL ACTIVITY 1

Table 18.1 shows the **labour force** and unemployment rate in six countries in 2017.

Table 18.1

Country	Labour force (millions)	Unemployment rate (%)
Afghanistan	8	35
Bangladesh	72	4
India	510	9
Myanmar	22	6
Pakistan	63	6
Sri Lanka	9	5

Using the information in Table 18.1:

a Which country had the highest number of people unemployed in 2017?

b How many people were employed in Bangladesh in 2017?

Does unemployment matter?

Unemployment does matter. With people out of work, we cannot enjoy as many goods and services as possible. For instance, some people may be homeless while there are unemployed building workers.

The government may have to provide support to the unemployed. This will involve an opportunity cost (see Chapter 4). For instance, the tax revenue spent on benefits for the unemployed could have been used to employ more teachers.

Tax revenue will also be less than it would be if more people were employed. When people are in work, they are likely to have higher incomes and spend more. Both incomes and spending are taxed.

Unemployment clearly matters to the unemployed. They will have a low or no income. They may lose confidence and may become depressed. Any skills they have may become outdated and this will make it harder for them to get another job.

Can governments reduce unemployment?

Reducing unemployment will increase a country's output and raise people's income. There are a number of measures a government can take to reduce unemployment. One is to provide good quality education and training. This may raise workers' skills, which may make it easier for them to find jobs. If firms are going out of business and there is not enough demand in the country, the government may try to increase spending in the country. It may do this by spending more itself or by cutting taxes so that its people can spend more.

DISCUSSION POINT

Should the government provide financial support to the unemployed?

GROUP ACTIVITY 2

Decide whether you think the following will increase or reduce unemployment in a country:

a a decrease in the information available about job vacancies

b a decrease in tourism in the country

c an increase in adult illiteracy

d an increase in the gap between house prices in different countries

e an increase in spending in the country.

DISCUSSION POINT

How will an economist's advice on the possible ways to reduce unemployment be influenced by her or his view on its cause?

Summary

In this chapter you have learned that:

- There are people who are willing and able to work who do not have jobs. They are unemployed.
- The unemployment rate is the number of people who are without a job and who are looking for one as a percentage of the labour force.
- The reasons why people may be unemployed include lacking skills employers want, not being able or willing to move to where the jobs are, being between jobs, being seasonally unemployed and there being a shortage of jobs available.
- Unemployment imposes costs on the economy. Output is lower than it could be, benefits may be provided by the government to the unemployed and tax revenue will be lower than possible.
- Unemployment harms the unemployed. Their income is likely to be low. They may lose confidence, become depressed and their skills may become out of date.
- The measures a government can take to reduce unemployment are improving education and training, spending more and cutting taxes.

End-of-chapter questions

1. Why do economists not classify the retired as unemployed?
2. A country has 40 million people in jobs and 5 million unemployed people. What is the size of the labour force?
3. Why do the skills people need to get a job change over time?
4. What would make it easier for people to move from one part of the country to another?
5. Why may a firm reduce the number of workers it employs?
6. Why are the living standards likely to be higher if unemployment is lower?
7. Why may government spending increase when there is unemployment?
8. Why do you think it becomes harder for people to find another job the longer they have been unemployed?
9. Why are well-educated people less likely to be unemployed than those who are less well-educated?
10. Why may cutting taxes reduce unemployment?

INDEPENDENT RESEARCH

Research the causes of youth unemployment. See, for example, 'Youth Unemployment: Causes and Solution' on the *Peace Child International* website.

Chapter 19
What jobs will we be doing in the future?

> **KEY TERM**
>
> **Self-employed:** someone who works for her or himself rather than for an employer. She or he may work on a contract basis or own her or his own firm.

Changing jobs

Amirah Alsharekh lives in Kuwait City in Kuwait. Her grandfather was a pearl fisherman. Her father works as senior manager for a major oil firm. Previously, he worked in management posts in two other oil firms. Amirah's mother became one of the first policewomen in the country when she took up her job in 2010. There are now more women in Kuwait's labour force than men.

Amirah's favourite subjects at school are economics, English and history. She would like to spend some of her working time teaching economics but she would also like to do some translating work and write historical fiction novels.

The jobs we are doing and how we are employed is changing. In the future, there is an increased possibility that people will work for more employers or be **self-employed** and will do a number of different jobs.

19.1 Police officer in Kuwait

> **KEY TERM**
>
> **Primary sector:** agriculture, fishing, forestry, mining and other industries that extract natural resources.

Different sectors

Industries and employment can be divided into the primary, secondary and tertiary sectors. The **primary sector** is where production starts. It covers agriculture, fishing, forestry, mining and extraction of oil. As economies develop, they become more efficient at, for instance, growing crops. As a result, they can produce more using fewer resources, so the number of workers employed in the primary sector tends to decline.

KEY TERMS

Secondary sector: manufacturing and construction.

Tertiary sector: services.

The **secondary sector** covers manufacturing and construction. At first, as incomes rise, more resources are usually devoted to producing goods and building houses, offices and factories. Then, while the output of the secondary sector rises, fewer, but more productive, workers are employed in this sector.

The **tertiary sector** is the service sector. This sector usually employs an increasing proportion of a country's workers. Demand for services tends to increase by more than demand for goods, as people's incomes rise, and increases in productivity in the other two sectors frees up workers to move to this sector. Kuwait has relied largely on oil production but now more and more of its resources are being devoted to the tertiary sector, particularly tourism and banking.

GROUP ACTIVITY 1

Decide whether the following jobs are in the primary, secondary or tertiary sectors:

a accountant

b car worker

c footballer

d nurse

e shepherd

f shipbuilder

g television reporter.

DISCUSSION POINT

In which sector do most of the people you know work?

Formal and informal economies

People work in the formal economy, also sometimes called the formal sector, when they have a long-term contract, defined working conditions, access to sickness payment and retirement pension, some degree of job security and are covered by any national minimum wage legislation. These workers usually work for one employer at a time and work relatively regular hours. In contrast, people work in the informal sector when they do not have a contract, have limited employment rights, irregular working hours and no permanent employer.

The informal economy has traditionally been associated with poor countries. Since the global financial crisis of 2008, there has been a growth of the informal economy in rich countries. Some of those made unemployed during the crisis took up a number of jobs for hourly payments. Advances in technology have fuelled the growth in the informal economy. It has made it easier for workers and firms to contact each other about work. The informal sector is now sometimes known as the gig economy. This gets its name from musicians doing a number of gigs.

There are a number of benefits that work in the informal sector can bring. Workers can decide when and where they want to work. They do, however, miss out on rights that those in the formal sector have such as sick pay, holiday pay, pensions and protection from unfair dismissal. Recently there have been a number of legal cases in the USA and Europe trying to establish whether particular groups of workers are self-employed, contracting out their labour or are really employees.

GROUP ACTIVITY 2

Which workers are most likely to be in the informal economy?

a casual farm workers

b cleaners

c delivery drivers

d surgeons

e writers.

Public and private sectors

KEY TERMS

Public sector: the part of the economy controlled by the government.

Private sector: the part of the economy covering firms owned by individuals and shareholders.

People work in the **public sector** when they work for the government. There may be a number of advantages working for the government, for example greater job security as the government may not want to increase unemployment. The government is more likely to enforce any national minimum wage legislation and legislation on, for instance, working hours. Public sector jobs also offer better pensions and longer holidays.

Some people, however, like working for the **private sector**. Some private sector firms may earn high revenue and so may be able to pay their workers high wages. It is also possible that workers may be able to be more creative, if the government is more rigid in how it requires its workers to carry out their duties.

In recent years, the proportion of people working in the public sector has declined in a number of countries. This is because governments have moved the production of some goods and services to the private sector.

DISCUSSION POINT

Would you rather work as a teacher in a government-run school or a privately run school?

Women's participation in the labour force

In most countries, a higher proportion of women are now working than in the past. The proportion of the country's labour force that is female tends to rise as the country's economic growth and development increases. There are, however, some poor countries where a high proportion of the labour force is already female. For instance, 55% of Mozambique's labour force and 50% of Angola's labour force are female. In these and some other poor countries, many of the female workers are doing low-paid jobs in the informal economy.

In recent years there has been a steady increase in the proportion of women working in some rich countries and a faster rise in some other rich countries. For instance, there has been a steady rise in the USA where women now account for 45% of the country's labour force. The rise is more dramatic in Saudi Arabia, although from a low base. In 2010, women accounted for 11% of the labour force. By 2018 this percentage had increased to 32%. Most countries welcome a rise in the proportion of women who work because it increases the output the country is capable of producing.

There are a number of reasons why more women are now working. These include:

- A rise in their qualifications. For instance, 52% of Saudi Arabian university students are now female.

- Changing social attitudes. More employers throughout the world are now prepared to employ females and treat them on equal terms with male employees.
- A rise in pay in some countries. The higher pay that women can now gain is encouraging more of them to work.
- A fall in the birth rate. Having fewer children makes it easier for women to work.
- Greater participation of men in childrearing. This is, again, making it easier, for women to work.
- A rise in tertiary employment. Working in the service sector usually involves less physical strength than, for instance, mining.

GROUP ACTIVITY 3

Decide which of the following are likely to encourage more women to work:

a an increase in the birth rate
b an increase in part-time employment
c a reduction in discrimination against women
d a reduction in the price of childcare.

Advances in technology

Some people are concerned that changes in technology may reduce the number of jobs available. For example, the introduction of driverless cars will reduce the demand for taxi drivers and delivery drivers. Advances in technology, however, not only destroy some jobs, they also create others. New jobs are created connected with new technology. For instance, there are now jobs in nanotechnology and robotics. Advances in technology also reduce the price of some products, such as cars and washing machines, while raising incomes. These effects increase people's ability to buy more goods and services. The higher demand results in more jobs. For instance, in many countries, there has been an increase in the number of jobs in the tourism industry.

What advances in technology are doing is putting an end to some physically hard, dangerous and boring jobs, and creating more jobs in the care and knowledge industries. Workers do, however, have to be adaptive, learning new skills.

Summary

In this chapter you have learned that:

- People are now unlikely to stay in the same job throughout their working life.
- As economies develop, employment in the primary sector tends to decline. It rises and then falls in the secondary sector. The tertiary sector usually continues to expand.
- Workers have more job security and rights in the formal economy.
- Recently, there has been a growth in the informal (gig) economy in some countries.
- There has been a growth in employment in the private sector in a number of countries as more production is now carried out by the private sector.
- More women are now working because of a rise in their qualifications, greater acceptance of women working, a fall in the birth rate, greater help of men with childrearing and a rise in tertiary employment.
- Advances in technology put an end to some jobs but also create other jobs.

End-of-chapter questions

1 Why might someone like working for the same employer for a long period of time?

2 Which sector – primary, secondary or tertiary – employs most workers in most rich countries?

3 Identify **two** advantages of working in the gig economy.

4 Why may it be difficult for someone in the gig economy to get a loan to buy a house?

5 Identify **two** possible benefits of working in the public sector.

6 What effect is a rise in the number of females going to university likely to have on university lecturers' pay?

7 What effect may a rise in the life expectancy of their parents have on women working?

8 How are self-checkouts in supermarkets affecting employment?

9 What effect is a rise in life expectancy having on the number of people employed as doctors and nurses?

10 Why is regular training of workers important?

INDEPENDENT RESEARCH

Find out how workers have to adapt to changes caused by advances in technology. See, for example, 'ICT: Changing work patterns' on the *BBC GCSE Bitesize* website.

Chapter 20
Why does the USA buy clothes from Pakistan?

International trade

Natalie Johnson got a job as a fashion retailer buyer for a major clothing store in the USA after completing a degree in economics and business studies. She analyses trends in the clothes people are buying, checks what competitors are selling and researches the best firms to buy clothes from. The last aspect of her job involves her attending trade fairs and visiting firms that produce clothing at home and abroad. Recently, her firm has agreed a contract with three Pakistani firms to supply a range of shirts, dresses and trousers.

KEY TERM

International trade: the exchange of goods and services between countries.

The exchange of goods and services between countries, known as **international trade**, has increased over the past 50 years. The USA, for instance, now sells approximately 14% of the products it produces to other countries and buys approximately 16% of what it consumes from other countries. International trade plays an even more important role for some other countries. For instance, Thailand sells more than two-thirds of its output abroad while buying nearly two-thirds of the goods and services it consumes from abroad.

The trade in clothing between the USA and Pakistan

KEY TERM

Imports: goods and services bought from other countries.

The USA produces clothing but also buys clothing from Pakistan. Products bought from other countries are known as **imports**. There are a number of reasons why US firms import clothing from Pakistan and other countries to sell to their customers. These include:

- competitive prices charged by Pakistani firms
- good quality Pakistani clothing
- variety in the form of different designs of Pakistani clothing.

US imports

As well as clothing, the USA also imports machinery, motor vehicle parts, computers and a range of other products. The main countries that the USA imports from are China, Canada, Mexico and Japan.

Changes in import expenditure

KEY TERM

Import expenditure: the total amount spent on goods and services bought from other countries.

The amount a country spends on imports may rise for a number of reasons including:

- An increase in incomes in the country. People will have more money to spend on both domestically produced products and imports.
- A rise in the prices of domestically produced products, This may make imports more internationally competitive.
- An increase in the quality of imports. This would make imports more desirable.

US exports

KEY TERMS

Specialisation: the concentration on a particular product or task.

Exports: goods and services sold to other countries.

Being able to import goods and services enables countries to specialise. They do not have to produce all the products they consume. They can concentrate on what they are best at producing. This is known as **specialisation**. They can then sell some of what they produce in exchange for imports.

Exports are goods and services sold to other countries. The USA exports a wide range of products including soybeans, corn, aircraft, cars, medical equipment, and banking, financial and insurance services.

The most important destinations of US exports are Canada, Mexico, China and Japan.

20.2 Container ship being loaded with goods in a US port

Changes in export revenue

KEY TERM

Export revenue: the total amount earned from selling goods and services to other countries.

The amount a country earns from selling exports may rise for a number of reasons including:

- An increase in incomes in other countries. Foreigners will have more money to spend on both domestically produced products and this country's exports.
- A fall in the prices of domestically produced products, This may make the country's exports more internationally competitive.
- An increase in the quality of exports. This would make the country's exports more desirable.

DISCUSSION POINT

Why do some countries both export and import cars?

GROUP ACTIVITY 1

Decide whether the following are Bangladeshi exports or Bangladeshi imports:

a French cars bought by Bangladeshi car distributors

b Bangladeshi grown rice sold to Myanmar

c Bangladeshi ships transporting Indian goods

d German-made machines purchased by Bangladeshi firms

e Indian shirts bought by Bangladeshi shops.

GROUP ACTIVITY 2

Use the World Factbook to research the following countries' main exports. From the World Factbook home page, select a country to view, and then click on 'Economy'. The sections, 'Agriculture – products' and 'Industries', list each country's main agricultural products and industries.Using Table 20.1, match each of the countries with one of their key exports.

Table 20.1

Country	Key export
Brazil	Cocoa
Chile	Copper
China	Milk
Cote d'Ivoire	Oil
New Zealand	Rubber
Saudi Arabia	Sugar
Thailand	Tea

KEY TERMS

Trade balance: a record of export revenue and import expenditure.

Balance of payments: a record of a country's economic transactions with other countries.

Trade surplus: export revenue exceeding import expenditure.

Trade deficit: import expenditure exceeding export revenue.

Trade balance

Governments keep records of export revenue and import expenditure. They publish this information in an account known as the **trade balance**. This is part of the country's **balance of payments**. The trade balance is export revenue minus import expenditure. If export revenue is greater than import expenditure, the country is said to have a **trade surplus**. If import expenditure exceeds export revenue, the country is said to have a **trade deficit**. The USA spends more on imported goods and services than it earns from exports of goods and services. In 2016, it had a trade deficit of $503 billion as it imported $2.712 billion worth of goods and services, and exported $2.209 billion worth of goods and services.

INDIVIDUAL ACTIVITY 1

Calculate, using the information from Table 20.2, whether the following countries had a trade deficit or a trade surplus in 2016.

Table 20.2 Five countries' exports and imports in 2016

Country	Exports ($ billion)	Imports ($ billion)
China	1900	1505
India	270	370
Japan	640	585
Mauritius	2.4	4.4
Pakistan	21	40

DISCUSSION POINT

What effect do you think the internet is having on trade between countries?

Summary

In this chapter you have learned that:

- The products we buy come from many different countries.
- Products the inhabitants of a country buy from abroad are called imports.
- Products may be brought from abroad because they are cheaper, better quality or have different features than those produced by domestic firms.
- Imports may increase because people have higher incomes, some of which they may spend on products from abroad. Other reasons for an increase in imports are a rise in the price of domestically produced products and a rise in the quality of imports.
- Exports are products the country's producers sell abroad.
- Exports may rise if incomes abroad increase, the price of exports falls or their quality rises.
- A trade deficit occurs when import expenditure is greater than export revenue.
- A trade surplus occurs when export revenue is greater than import revenue.
- The trade balance is part of a country's balance of payments.

End-of-chapter questions

1 What is the difference between imports and exports?

2 What is the connection between international trade and specialisation?

3 Do countries export both goods and services?

4 Why may the price of imports fall and import expenditure rise?

5 How do consumers benefit from international trade?

6 Why might an increase in incomes in a country reduce that country's exports?

7 What effect would you expect a fall in transport costs to have on the volume of international trade?

8 What is the difference between a trade deficit and a trade surplus?

9 If a country has a trade deficit of $8 billion and its export revenue is $24 billion, what is its import expenditure?

10 Why would the sale of tyres by a German firm to a German car producer not appear in Germany's balance of payments?

INDEPENDENT RESEARCH

Using the World Factbook for your country, find out the main goods your country exports and imports and what are the main countries it exports to and imports from.

Refer back to Group activity 2, which will remind you of how to search for this information

Chapter 21

Why does the Indian firm Tata produce cars, steel and salt in the UK?

KEY TERM

Multinational company: a firm that has its headquarters in one country but produces in a number of countries.

Multinational companies

Ajay Gupta's father works for the Tata Group, a large Indian **multinational company** (MNC). Ajay would like to work for Tata as an economist. One reason he would like to work for the firm is that he may be able to work in other countries. Tata Group has its headquarters in Mumbai, India. It operates more than 100 firms in more than 100 countries. In the UK, they include Jaguar Land Rover, which produces cars, Tata Steel and Tata Chemicals which, among other products, produces salt.

Why does Tata produce in other countries?

KEY TERMS

Government subsidies: payments by the government to encourage the production or consumption of a product.

Trade restrictions: any government policy that limits imports and exports.

Among the reasons Tata and other MNCs produce in other countries are:

- Lower labour costs. This may be because the labour in the countries is skilled and can produce a high output per hour. In some lower-income countries, it may be because the wage rates are low.
- A growing market in the countries. If incomes are rising in the countries, the MNC may be able to sell many products in the countries.
- **Government subsidies**. The governments of the countries may give the firm some money to set up in the country.
- To get around **trade restrictions**. Producing in the countries means that the MNC will not have to pay the taxes that the governments impose on imports. It will also not be affected by any limits the government puts on the number of imports that can come into the country.
- Access to raw materials. In some cases, MNCs set up in a country in order to be able to, for instance, mine copper.

GROUP ACTIVITY 1

You are in charge of an MNC in the following industries. In each case, research in which of the countries given you would open a new firm and explain why:

a the film industry – India, Malaysia or Myanmar

b the gold mining industry – France, Poland or Russia

c the ship building industry – China, Kazakhstan or Switzerland.

Do countries benefit from the presence of foreign MNCs?

Foreign MNCs may bring both advantages and disadvantages to a country.

Advantages of foreign MNCs to a country

- An increase in the number of jobs in the country. MNCs may employ local workers. This may reduce the number of unemployed people in the country.
- MNCs may pay higher wages than domestic firms. This would enable the workers to buy more goods and services.

KEY TERM

Infrastructure: the facilities that make economic activity possible, including electricity, roads and rail.

- MNCs may train workers. This may enable the workers to get promoted posts with the MNCs or better jobs with domestic firms should they leave the MNCs.
- An improvement in the country's **infrastructure**. For instance, MNCs may build roads and docks that can be used by domestic firms.
- An increase in government tax revenue. MNCs may pay taxes on the profits they earn in the country.
- The introduction of new technology and management techniques. MNCs may bring in new ideas, new machinery and new methods that domestic firms may learn from.

21.1 Copper mining in Zambia

Disadvantages of foreign MNCs to a country

- Depletion of resources. An MNC, for instance, may mine all the country's copper quickly, leaving no copper for future generations.
- Pollution. An MNC may set up in another country to get round tight anti-pollution laws in its own country.
- Profit may be sent out of the country back to the MNC's country of origin. The motive behind this may be to avoid paying taxes in the countries it is producing in.
- MNCs may drive domestic firms out of business. If the domestic firms are producing the same products, they may not be able to compete with possibly larger firms. In this case, MNCs may not increase the country's output, just who produces it.
- Pressure may be put on governments to give the MNCs favourable treatment. The output of some MNCs is larger than the output of some countries. This gives them considerable power. They may use this power to persuade governments to introduce measures that will benefit the MNCs but not necessarily the country's workers and consumers. For instance, an MNC may put pressure on a government to remove restrictions on the number of hours a week a worker can be made to work and safety standards on products.

GROUP ACTIVITY 2

Discuss which MNCs you would allow to set up firms in your country:

a an MNC that produces parts used in the production of cars made by your country's car producers

b an MNC that processes nuclear waste

c an MNC that plans to open a training centre for the bank staff it will employ in your country

d an MNC that uses advanced technology and produces a product made by firms already in your country.

Why is the number of MNCs increasing?

More firms are producing outside their home country. The reasons for this include:

- Improvements in communications. Advances in technology make it easier for those running MNCs to keep in contact with their staff in other countries.
- Reductions in transport costs. This makes it cheaper to send product parts and staff between countries.
- Greater similarity of tastes. For instance, people throughout the world use smartphones and people watch some of the same television programmes.

DISCUSSION POINT

What would attract an MNC to set up in your country?

Summary

In this chapter you have learned that:

- Multinational companies, such as Tata, produce in a number of countries.
- MNCs gain a number of advantages from producing in other countries. These may include lower labour costs, a growing market for its products in the country, government subsidies, getting round trade restrictions and access to raw materials.
- The advantages a country may gain from the presence of foreign MNCs may include increased number of jobs, higher wages, more trade, improvement of the country's infrastructure, rise in tax income and the introduction of new technology and management techniques.
- The possible disadvantages a country may experience as a result of the presence of foreign MNCs are depletion of resources, pollution, profit being sent out of the country, pressure being put on the government to treat the MNCs on favourable terms and some domestic firms going out of business.
- Improvements in communications, growing similarities of tastes and reduction in transport costs are increasing the number of MNCs.

End-of-chapter questions

1. Why is Tata classified as an Indian MNC rather than a UK MNC?
2. If an MNC pays workers a lower wage than it pays in its home country, will the workers benefit?
3. Why does the existence of raw materials, such as rubber, encourage an MNC to set up in a country?
4. If an MNC creates an additional 2000 jobs in a country, will this necessarily reduce unemployment in its home country by 2000?
5. Why may an MNC build roads in a country it locates in?
6. How may domestic firms benefit from the presence of MNCs?
7. Why is the depletion of its resources a disadvantage for a country?
8. Why may an MNC pollute more in other countries than in its home country?
9. Why may an MNC be able to put pressure on a government?
10. Why is the number of foreign MNCs in China likely to increase in the future?

INDEPENDENT RESEARCH

Research the reasons for MNCs and their advantages and disadvantages. See, for example, 'Multinational organisations' on the *BBC Higher Bitesize* website.

The outbreak of a possible trade war

KEY TERM

Import tariff: a tax imposed on imports.

Pamelina Aldo was worried in 2018 that both her father and mother would lose their jobs because of what the US government was planning to do. The US President had announced that a 25% **import tariff** would be put on imports of steel and a 10% tariff on aluminium. Brazil is a major producer and exporter of steel. Pamelina's father works in a Brazilian steel mill. If it sells less steel, it may cut production and dismiss some of its workers.

Pamelina's mother is employed by a shipping firm that transports US exports of cars to Brazil. If the Brazilian government responds to the US tariffs by imposing tariffs on US products, there will be less demand for transport between the two countries and Pamelina's mother may lose her job.

22.1 A steel plant in Brazil

Trade wars

KEY TERM

Trade restrictions: barriers to international trade.

A trade war occurs when two or more countries increase their **trade restrictions** in retaliation for each other's trade restrictions. For example, country A may impose a tariff of 10% on imports from country B. In response, country B imposes a tariff of 10% on country A's imports. Then country A reacts by increasing its tariff to 15% and country B raises its by 18%. This situation could escalate further.

The weapons used in a trade war

KEY TERM

Import quota: a limit on imports.

There are a number of trade restrictions that a government could use. As well as tariffs, a government could use, for instance, quotas and embargoes. An **import quota** is a limit on the amount of a good that the government allows to be imported from another country.

KEY TERM

Import embargo: a ban on imports.

An **import embargo** is an extreme form of quota, as it is a complete ban on imports or on imports of a particular product.

DISCUSSION POINT

Do you think it is ever justified for a government to ban the import of a product?

GROUP ACTIVITY 1

Which of the following measures could a government use to restrict imports?

- **a** complex forms that have to be filled out when importing products
- **b** limits on the amount of foreign currency available
- **c** quality standards
- **d** subsidies given to domestic producers.

Why do trade wars break out?

Trade wars break out because governments want to protect their industries and to prevent unemployment. They often come under pressure from those domestic industries that are facing increasing competition from imports. The domestic industries and their governments will often claim that these industries need protection because of unfair foreign competition. For instance, the government of country A may argue that the government of country B is subsidising its industries or that some firms in country B are engaging in what is known as **dumping**. Such unfair competition, the government of country A may argue, could drive its industries out of business, resulting in workers losing their jobs. Indeed, firms in country B may engage in dumping with the specific intention of eliminating competitors from country A, so that when they have captured country A's market they can raise the price they charge. Such claims are difficult to prove.

KEY TERM

Dumping: selling products in a foreign market at below the cost of production.

GROUP ACTIVITY 2

Decide which would reduce the likelihood of a trade war breaking out:

- **a** a greater awareness that trade wars can make everyone poorer
- **b** a rise in countries' income
- **c** growing suspicion by a government that other countries' firms are lowering their prices to stop its firms selling in their markets
- **d** the signing of international trade agreements.

The effects of trade wars

Trade wars are likely to result in all the participant countries losing. Among the negative effects that may result are:

- Higher prices for consumers. Tariffs and quotas usually increase prices. The sellers of products that have tariffs imposed on them are likely to raise prices to maintain their profits. Quotas, by reducing the supply of imports, are also likely to raise prices.

- Less choice for consumers. If fewer products are imported, there will be less for consumers to select from.
- Quality of the products produced may fall. Less competition may result in firms feeling less pressure to raise the quality of the products they produce.
- Higher costs for some domestic firms. If trade restrictions are imposed on imported raw materials and machinery, it is likely to make it more expensive for domestic firms to produce their products. For example, if a government imposes a tariff on foreign-produced cotton, its firms that produce clothing may switch to buying domestically produced cotton. If most firms producing clothing did not buy domestically produced cotton before, it is likely that this is because it was more expensive than imported cotton.
- Reduced output. Trade restrictions will mean that countries will not be able to concentrate on producing what they are best at. Some products may be produced by less-efficient producers.

GROUP ACTIVITY 3

Decide which would benefit from the US government imposing a tariff on Brazilian steel:

a Brazilian firms that sell insurance to the Brazilian steel industry

b Brazilian steel workers

c US car producers

d US MNCs producing in Brazil.

Summary

In this chapter you have learned that:

- Trade wars break out when governments impose trade restrictions in retaliation for other governments imposing trade restrictions.
- Among the measures a government may use in a trade war are tariffs, quotas and embargoes.
- Trade wars break out because of pressure on governments to protect domestic industries and employment and because it may be suspected that the governments and firms of other countries are engaging in unfair competition.
- Trade wars result in higher prices and less choice for consumers.
- Trade wars increase the costs of production of some domestic firms.
- Global output is likely to be reduced as a result of a trade war.

End-of-chapter questions

1 Name three major steel producing countries.

2 What is the difference between a tariff and a quota?

3 Apart from restricting imports, why else may a government impose a tariff on imports?

4 Is charging a lower price always unfair competition?

5 Why is a subsidy sometimes described as a 'weapon' in a trade war?

6 Do consumers benefit from trade wars?

7 Do domestic firms benefit as a result of a trade war?

8 Why may training workers be a better approach to increased competition from abroad than engaging in a trade war?

9 Why is it more surprising that the USA has increased tariffs on Chinese products than on Brazilian products?

10 Does the world benefit from a trade war?

INDEPENDENT RESEARCH

Research why it is not easy to win a trade war. See, for example, 'Five reasons why trade wars aren't easy to win' on the *BBC News* website.

Chapter 23
Which country will have the strongest economy in 2050?

Forecasting

Stephanie Obasa is studying IGCSE Economics in Nigeria. She would like to go on to study economics at university and then to become an economist. She is particularly interested in forecasting the future economic performance of countries. Economists predict what will happen to, for example, countries' inflation rates, unemployment rates, trade in goods and services and output.

Stephanie has read that economists working for the National Bureau of Statistics are forecasting that Nigeria's output will increase by 5.6% in 2019 and that the country's inflation rate will be 8.5%.

23.1 Lagos, Nigeria

The strongest economy

The strongest economy is usually taken to be the one with the highest output. Table 23.1 shows the ten countries with the highest output in 2017 when world output was $78 trillion.

Table 23.1 The top ten countries in terms of output, 2017

Position	Country	Output ($ trillion)
1	USA	19.5
2	China	12.0
3	Japan	4.8
4	Germany	3.4
5	UK	2.6
6	India	2.5
7	France	2.4
8	Brazil	2.1
9	Italy	1.8
10	Canada	1.6

These ten countries accounted for two-thirds of global output in 2017. Output can be measured in a number of ways and according to one measure, China contributed more to global output than the USA.

KEY TERMS

Economic growth: an increase in a country's output.

Economic growth rate: the percentage increase in a country's output.

Economic growth

In the nineteenth century, the UK produced a higher output than the USA. Towards the end of the century and at the start of the twentieth century, the UK's output increased more slowly than that of the USA. Economists call an increase in a country's output **economic growth**. They name the percentage increase in a country's output, its **economic growth rate**. Figure 23.1 compares the economic growth rate of the six largest economies in recent years.

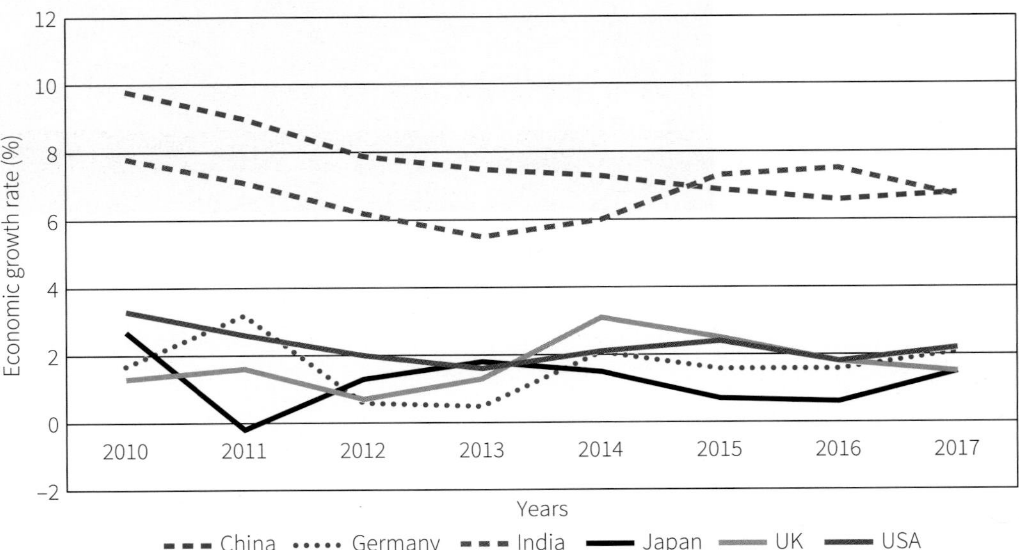

Fig. 23.1 The economic growth rate of the top six countries, 2010–2017

Prediction for 2050

While the USA was the largest economy in the twentieth century, accounting for more than 40% of global output, many economists are predicting that China will be the dominant economy in the twenty-first century. China is predicted by most economists to have the highest output in 2050. Some economists, however, suggest that India may be the top economy in 2050. This is because India's population and labour force are expected to be greater than China's and because the skills of India's workers are increasing at a fast rate.

GROUP ACTIVITY 1

Some economists are predicting that Indonesia, Mexico and Russia will soon appear in the list of top ten economies.

a What do these three economies have in common, which could explain why they may have a high output?

b Explain why countries seek to increase their output.

Strength

The country producing the highest output is likely to be a powerful and influential one. Its government is likely to play an important role in international organisations, such as the International Monetary Fund. What happens to its economic performance may have a significant influence on the global economy. This is because it may import and export on a large scale. It may have foreign MNCs in its economy, due to the large size of its market and MNCs from the country are likely to be operating throughout the world (see Chapter 21).

Output per head of population

The country with the highest output is likely to play a key role in the global economy. Some economists, however, argue that it is more important to look at countries in terms of output per head (output divided by population). This is because it is obvious that countries with larger populations are likely to produce a higher output than those with smaller populations. A country with a high output per head may or may not have much international power but its people will enjoy a high number of goods and services.

Table 23.2 shows the ten countries with the highest output per head in 2017.

Table 23.2 The top ten countries in terms of output per head 2017

Position	Country	Output per head ($)
1	Qatar	130 000
2	Luxembourg	102 000
3	Singapore	88 100
4	Brunei	79 700
5	Kuwait	71 000
6	Ireland	69 500
7	Norway	69 000
8	UAE	67 700
9	San Marino	64 500
10	Switzerland	60 200

GROUP ACTIVITY 2

Table 23.3 shows the five African countries with the highest output in 2017. Using information from the table, calculate each of the five African countries' output per head.

Table 23.3

Position	Country	Output ($ millions)	Population (millions)
1	Nigeria	437 000	190
2	South Africa	427 500	57
3	Egypt	372 400	98
4	Algeria	266 500	41
5	Morocco	180 000	36

Quality of life

In assessing which is the best performing country, economists are increasingly arguing that more than output and output per head should be considered. Each year, the United Nations (UN) publishes a Human Development Report in which it discusses the progress countries are making in improving the quality of its citizens' lives. It also ranks countries in an index, called the Human Development Index (HDI) that takes account of income per head (which is equivalent to output per head), education its citizens receive and life expectancy. Table 23.4 shows the top ten countries in the UN's Human Development Report 2016.

Table 23.4 The ten countries with the highest HDI ranking in the 2016 HDI Report

HDI ranking	Country
1	Norway
2	Australia
3	Switzerland
4	Germany
5	Denmark
6	Singapore
7	Netherlands
8	Ireland
9	Iceland
10	Canada

People's quality of life is affected by more than the goods and services they consume, the education they receive and how long they live. Indeed, it is influenced by a wide range of factors. For this reason, economists are developing a number of other ways of measuring countries' performance.

GROUP ACTIVITY 3

Decide which would be likely to increase and which would be likely to decrease the quality of people's lives:

a a decrease in traffic congestion
b a decrease in loneliness
c an increase in leisure time
d an increase in pollution
e an increase in stress at work.

DISCUSSION POINT

How can economics improve the quality of people's lives?

Summary

In this chapter you have learned that:

- Strong economies have high output.
- Ten countries accounted for more than two-thirds of global output in 2017.
- A country's economic growth rate is the percentage increase in its output.
- It is predicted that either China or India will have the largest output in 2050.
- Producing a high output can give a country economic power.
- The growth of a country's output can benefit other countries by, for instance, the country importing more and by providing markets for foreign MNCs.
- People's quality of life is influenced by a number of factors including the goods and services they consume, the education they receive and how long they live.

End-of-chapter questions

1 Why do countries aim for a high output?

2 What does it mean if an economy's economic growth rate falls from 5% to 3%?

3 What would it mean if a country has a negative economic growth rate?

4 Why may India have the highest output in 2050?

5 How could a country have a rise in output without any increase in employment?

6 Will everyone in a country benefit from a rise in its output?

7 How may the growth of the Chinese economy benefit, for instance, Malaysia?

8 Why may a country with a large output have a low output per head?

9 Why may a country have a low output per head but a high HDI?

10 What effect would a fall in working hours be likely to have on the quality of people's lives?

INDEPENDENT RESEARCH

Using the Human Development Index (HDI), find out where your country comes in the rankings and produce a list of the top ten countries and bottom ten countries in terms of education. To find this, navigate to the *Human Development Report* website.

In the Human Development Data (1990–2015) Dimension box, select Education. Then in the Education box, select Education Index to bring up a list of countries with their HDI ranking.

SECTION 3
Important numbers, organisations and economists

The numbers that economists use regularly are described below.

Averages

Economists calculate a number of averages. They calculate average total cost and average revenue. Average total cost is total cost divided by output and average revenue is total revenue divided by total sales (see Chapter 9). Economists also calculate, for instance, average wages and average hours worked.

Index numbers

An index number is a figure that compares, for instance, prices, output or wages with a base value. The base value is set at 100. Index numbers have the advantage of making it easy to compare figures over time. For instance, if the price level was given a base value in 2018 and then it is 106 in 2019, it is clear to see that, on average, prices have risen by 6% between 2018 and 2019.

Percentages

For example, economists calculate percentage changes in price, demand and supply. A rise in price from \$10 to \$16 would be a 60% increase $\left(\frac{\$6}{\$10} \times 100\right)$.

The birth rate

This is the number of live births per thousand of the population per year. A birth rate of 8 would mean that 8 babies had been born for every 1000 people in the population.

Budget balance

This is the difference between tax revenue and government spending. A budget surplus means tax revenue is greater than government spending. In contrast, a budget deficit means government spending is greater than tax revenue.

The death rate

This is the number of people who die per thousand of the population per year. A death rate of 6 would mean that a country with a population of 3 million would have experienced

$$\frac{3\,000\,000}{1000} \times 6 = 18\,000 \text{ deaths}$$

that year.

The exchange rate

This is the price of one currency in terms of another currency. For instance, the price of a US dollar may be 110 Pakistani rupees. This would mean that a Pakistani good with a price of 6380 rupees would sell for \$58 $\left(\frac{6380}{110}\right)$ in the USA.

Gross domestic product (GDP)

This is the country's total output. It is also equal to the total income and total expenditure in the country.

GDP per head

This is the country's output divided by the country's population. It is also sometimes called GDP per capita.

The inflation rate

This is the percentage rise in the price level of a country. An annual inflation rate of 5% would mean that, on average, prices are 5% higher this year than last year.

Net migration

This is the number of people who come into the country minus the number of people who leave the country to live elsewhere. Net emigration means that more people are leaving than entering the country. More people coming into the country than leaving is called net immigration.

Population size

This is the number of people living in a country. The population size of countries varies significantly. For instance, in 2018 Tuvalu had a population of 11 700 while China had a population of 1 400 000 000 (1.4 billion).

The trade in goods and services balance

This is the value of exports of goods and services minus the value of imports of goods and services. A trade in goods surplus means export revenue is greater than import expenditure. In contrast, a budget deficit occurs when import expenditure is greater than export revenue.

The unemployment rate

This is calculated by dividing the number of people unemployed by the total number of people in the labour force (employed and unemployed). The formula for calculating the unemployment rate is:

$$\frac{\text{Unemployed}}{\text{Labour force}} \times 100$$

Chapter 25

Important economic institutions, markets and organisations

There are a number of key economic institutions, markets and organisations that you will come across in your studies.

Banks

These are also called commercial banks. They move money from those who have more money than they want to spend now to those who want to spend more than they have. They accept deposits of money from people who want to save and lend to those who want to borrow. They provide a number of ways for deposit holders to make payments, including direct debits. They also provide a range of financial services including changing foreign currency into the domestic currency and insurance.

Central banks

A central bank controls the country's banking system. It is the government's bank and the bank used by commercial banks. It issues banknotes, sets interest rates and controls the amount of money in the economy. The oldest central bank is Sweden's Riksbank, which was founded in 1668. Among the best known central banks are the Bank of England, the Federal Reserve Bank (USA), the People's Bank of China and the Reserve Bank of India.

Commodity markets

These are markets where primary products are bought and sold. Commodity markets include 'soft commodities', which are agricultural products. These include coffee, cocoa, corn, cotton, milk, rice, sugar, tea and wheat. Commodity markets also include 'hard commodities'. These are products that are mined or extracted, including copper, gold, nickel, silver and oil.

Firms

Firms are businesses. They produce products, employ workers and buy machines. Some firms are small, based in one place and owned by one person. Other firms are very large, with branches found throughout the world. Large firms may own a high number of offices, factories or shops.

Firms can be grouped into industries. An industry consists of the firms that produce the same product. The furniture industry consists of firms that make, for instance, chairs, desks and cabinets.

Foreign exchange markets

These are arrangements that bring the buyers and sellers of countries' currencies into contact. Commercial banks, central banks and currency traders buy and sell currencies. Different currencies are bought and sold on foreign exchange markets throughout the world.

In 2018, the four currencies that were traded the most were the US dollar, the euro, the Japanese yen and the UK pound.

A foreign exchange market is also sometimes known as forex. People and institutions buy foreign exchange for a number of reasons, including to use it to buy goods and services in other countries, to set up factories, offices and shops in other countries, to influence the value of the domestic currency and to speculate. The top three places where foreign currencies were traded in 2018 were London, New York and Singapore.

Governments

Governments play an important role in the economy. They impose taxes and spend money on, for instance, education. Changes in taxes and government spending can influence the economy in a number of ways. For example, an increase in government spending on road building will increase the number of jobs in the country and may reduce transport costs. The imposition of a tax on soft drinks that contain a high amount of sugar may encourage people to switch to healthier drinks.

Housing market

In any country, the supply of housing comes from new builds and from any part of the stock of housing that is offered for sale. Demand for housing is influenced by a number of factors including population size, number of households, income, interest rate and the availability of loans. The housing market can be divided according to who provides it and the type of housing. There is public sector housing and private sector housing. There are also sub-markets for houses and apartments, for example.

Industries

An industry consists of all the firms that produce the same product. For example, the Japanese car industry includes Toyota, Honda, Nissan and the other firms that make cars in Japan. Industries can be classified in narrow or broad geographical terms. For example, the Japanese car industry includes fewer firms than the global car industry. Industries can be also classified at different levels according to the product. For instance, the Japanese micro sports car industry has fewer firms than the Japanese car industry.

International Monetary Fund (IMF)

The IMF was set up in 1945 and has its headquarters in Washington, DC, USA. It has a number of aims including promoting high employment and economic growth and reducing poverty. Its main aims are to encourage the growth of international trade and to ensure that countries can make and receive payments from each other. To achieve these last two aims, it helps countries that get into debt with other countries by importing more than they export.

25.1 The International Monetary Fund in Washington, DC, USA

Labour markets

In a labour market, workers supply their labour and employers demand their labour. In any country, the labour market can be divided into sub-markets. These include the markets for skilled and unskilled workers. There are markets for primary, secondary and tertiary sector workers and for particular occupations such as the market for plumbers.

Trade unions

A trade union is an organisation that represents workers. It negotiates with employers to improve its members' pay and working conditions and protect their jobs.

Trade unions sometimes take industrial action in support of their aims. The best known form of industrial action is a strike. This involves workers stopping work to put pressure on their employer to, for instance, agree to a wage rise or not make some of them redundant.

World Bank

The formal name for the World Bank is the International Bank for Reconstruction and Development. It was founded in 1947 and, like the IMF, has its headquarters in Washington DC, USA. Its key function now is to promote the development of low-income countries. It provides advice and funds for projects improving, for example, education, health and infrastructure.

Chapter 26
Famous economists

William Petty (1623–1687)

Place of birth: Romsey, UK.

Key areas of interest: William Petty was interested in how an economy works and how economic ideas can improve the quality of people's lives. He developed a number of economic terms, including full employment, and described the benefits of workers specialising and how an initial increase in government spending can result in a larger final increase in spending in an economy. He used statistics in his study of the economy and recognised the importance of measuring a country's output.

Interesting facts: William Petty left school at 13 and went to sea as a cabin boy. He then worked in a number of different jobs including being a medical doctor, a land surveyor, a member of parliament and a professor of music, as well as an economist. He was also an inventor. Among his inventions was an early form of toilet and a twin-hulled boat.

Thorstein Veblen (1857–1929)

Place of birth: Wisconsin, USA.

Key areas of interest: Thorstein Veblen combined the study of economics with psychology and sociology. He wrote about how some rich people in the USA spend money on some items, such as expensive cars and houses, mainly to show how wealthy they are. He called this 'conspicuous consumption'.

Interesting facts: Thorstein Veblen taught at a number of US universities. His students had mixed views about him. He spoke so quietly in lectures that many students could not hear him. However well his students had done, he gave almost all of them C grades. He also did not wash very often and rarely cleaned his teeth.

John Maynard Keynes (1883–1946)

Place of birth: Cambridge, UK.

Key areas of interest: Keynes' main interest was in macroeconomics and advising governments and international organisations on how to improve countries' macroeconomic performance. He recommended that governments should increase government spending to reduce large-scale unemployment. He explained how this could work his book *The General Theory of Employment, Interest and Money*, published in 1936. This is one of the most famous economics books.

Interesting facts: Keynes used to spend quite a lot of time in bed. He was not sleeping. He was working on his economic theories and studying the financial markets. He made a lot of money both for himself and for his college, Kings College, Cambridge. He had a wide range of interests, including painting and plays. He helped to found the Arts Theatre in Cambridge.

Joan Robinson (1903–1983)

Born: Surrey, UK.

Key areas of interest: Joan Robinson was a supporter of the ideas of John Maynard Keynes and was one of a group of economists who helped him to spread those ideas. She wrote about unemployment and economic growth. She is also known for her work on how firms compete. She examined, for instance, how they try to make their products appear different from those of their rivals.

Interesting facts: Joan Robinson regularly visited China and India and, in her later years, dressed mostly in Indian dress. She enjoyed debating ideas with both fellow professors and students. She supported a number of student protests at Cambridge University and took part in several student sit-ins.

Elinor Ostrom (1933–2012)

Born: California, USA.

Key areas of interest: Elinor Ostrom studied how people share what are sometimes called common resources such as fish, forests and rivers. She argued that people can manage these resources well and will avoid their overuse without the need for government intervention.

Interesting facts: Elinor Ostrom conducted field studies. For instance, she interviewed Indonesian fisherman and asked them how they limited how many fish they caught. To date, Elinor Ostrom has been the only woman to win the Nobel Prize in economics.

Amartya Sen (1933–)

Born: Santiniketan, India.

Key areas of interest: Amartya Sen has done pioneering work on the causes of poverty, famine and income inequality. He argues, for example, that famines are not usually caused by floods and droughts. Indeed, he thinks that famines are not the result of a general shortage of food but the result of some people not being able to afford enough food.

Interesting facts: Amartya Sen was born on a university campus and has since taught at some of the most prestigious universities in India, the UK and USA. In 1998 he won the Nobel Prize in economics.

Mahbub ul Haq (1934–1998)

Born: Punjab, Pakistan.

Key areas of interest: Mahbub ul Haq concentrated his studies on how countries, particularly low-income countries, could increase their citizens' choices and provide them with a better quality of life. He argued that the quality of people's lives is determined by more than the goods and services they consume. As well as undertaking economic research, he worked as the chief economist of Pakistan's Planning Commission, director of the Policy Planning Department of the World Bank and a special adviser to the United Nations.

Interesting facts: Mahbub ul Haq started the Human Development Report in 1990 and he devised the Human Development Index. The UN gives the Mahbub ul Haq Award for outstanding contribution to human development in his honour.

Muhammad Yunus (1940–)

Born: Chittagong, Bangladesh.

Key areas of interest: Muhammed Yunus has pioneered giving small loans to the poor on accessible terms to help them start and develop small businesses. Banks in the past have not always been willing to lend the poor. Muhammed Yunus has both explained the economic case for providing microfinance to the poor to help them, and others escape poverty, and has been involved in providing loans to the poor.

Interesting facts: Muhammed Yunus is both an academic and a banker. In 2006, he was awarded the Nobel Peace Prize for promoting economic and social development by founding the Grameen Bank. This bank for the poor has inspired the foundation of other microfinance banks in many other countries.

Thomas Piketty (1971–)

Born: Clichy, France.

Key areas of interest: The focus of Thomas Piketty's work is income and wealth inequality. He argues that wealth and income tend to become more unevenly distributed over time. He suggests this happens because the return the rich get from their shares and property increases at a more rapid rate than the growth in wages, particularly low wages.

Interesting fact: Thomas Piketty's book *Capital in the Twenty-First Century* is about wealth and income inequality in Europe and the USA since the eighteenth century. It was published in 2013, and is an international bestseller. It has sold more than ten million copies, making its author a wealthy man.

SECTION 4
Suggested answers to activities

Suggested answers

Chapter 4

Individual and group activity 1

a It is likely that your parents will have left school at a later age than your grandparents.

b You are likely to be leaving school at a later age than your parents and grandparents. Over time, in most countries, the school leaving age has been increasing.

Group activities

2 Examples of possible answers:

- **a** to study Business Studies
- **b** to go on holiday in Goa in India
- **c** to become a teacher
- **d** to print economics books
- **e** to spend money on healthcare.

3 Private benefits: a, c and d These are benefits received by patients who are consumers of healthcare.
External benefits: b and e. These are benefits received by people who are not patients or people working in healthcare at the time.

End-of-chapter questions

1 It means that students now have to be older before they can leave school.

2 The art teacher may have given up the opportunity to work as an artist.

3 Opportunity cost is an important concept in economics because economics explores the choices we make and the consequences of those choices.

4 Some children in poor countries leave school at a young age because their families cannot afford to keep them at school and because they need them to support the family by working.

5 People who leave school at a later age usually earn more than those who left earlier because they are likely to have more qualifications and more skills. Employers like to recruit well-qualified and skilled workers.

6 The friends you may make at school are a private benefit. You are consuming education and friendships are a benefit you may receive.

7 Social benefits minus private benefits is equal to external benefits.

8 When a government is deciding whether to raise the school leaving age, it should base its decision on social benefit. This is because it should take into account the full benefit, both to those involved in education and to other people.

9 If ten workers produce output valued at \$600 in two hours, their productivity is

$$\frac{\$600}{10} = \frac{\$60}{2} = \$30$$

On average, each worker produces an output valued at \$30 per hour.

10 Productivity has increased in most countries in the past 20 years for three main reasons. Workers are better educated, better trained and use better equipment due to advances in technology.

Chapter 5

Individual activities

1 **a** 32

b \$38

2

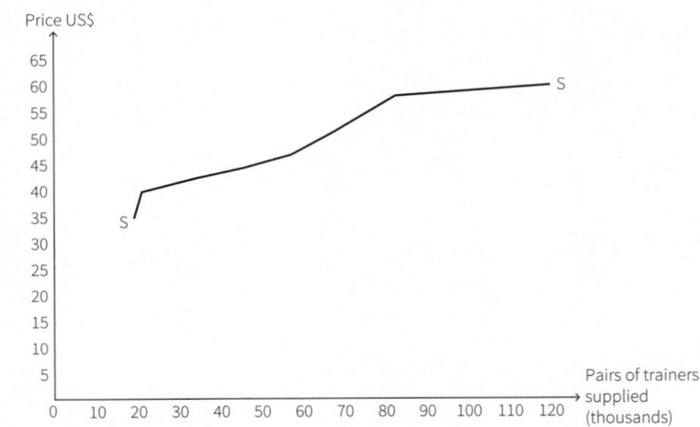

Group activities

1 **a** car travel

b tea

c nylon shirts

d pineapple juice

e cabbage.

End-of-chapter questions

1 Advertising and the association of certain qualities with brand names makes branded products so popular.
2 People's ability to buy a product is influenced by their income and by the prices of the products.
3 The price and availability of substitutes influences people's willingness to buy a product. For example, if a substitute to the product becomes cheaper, people are likely to become less willing to buy this product.
4 Price and quantity demanded are shown on a demand schedule.
5 A rise in price will cause a fall in demand. Price and demand move in opposite directions.
6 Demand is the willingness and ability to buy a product, whereas supply is the willingness and ability to sell a product. Demand moves in the opposite direction to price, whereas supply moves in the same direction.
7 Price is on the vertical axis of demand and supply diagrams.
8 It is profit that motivates firms to supply goods and services. Firms hope to receive more in revenue from the sale of their products than it costs them to produce the products.
9 A rise in price enables firms to cover the cost of supplying more trainers.
10 If shops are running out of trainers to sell, price will rise. Consumers will be competing with each other to get the trainers and some will be willing and able to pay higher prices.

Chapter 6

Individual activities

1 Increase/decrease in wages and suggested reason why:

Construction workers: Increase. Demand for housing would rise and so demand for construction workers would increase.

Cricket players: Increase. Cricket clubs would earn more revenue and so would be able to offer higher wages to attract the best players.

Dentists: Increase. Fewer people are likely to want to become dentists. The decrease in supply will drive up the wages of dentists.

Shop assistants: Decrease. Demand for shop assistants will decrease.

Taxi drivers: Decrease. Demand for taxi drivers will decrease.

University lecturers: Increase. More lecturers will be taken on.

Group activities

1 Increase: a, c and e as the club is likely to receive more revenue. In the case of a, more money will be received from the TV firms. In the case of c and e, more revenue is likely to be earned from extra ticket sales.

Reduce: b and d. Both are likely to result in fewer people wanting to watch the team play. The club is also likely to receive less TV coverage in a lower league.

2 **a** Head teachers. They are likely to have more experience and responsibility than teachers. They may also have higher qualifications.

b Lawyers. They will have higher qualifications than bus drivers and will be in shorter supply.

c Architects. They will have higher qualifications and be in shorter supply than window cleaners.

d TV presenters may have special skills and some may be very popular. Hotel cleaners are likely to be in higher supply relative to the demand for their labour.

e Opticians. Qualifications, gained after years of study, are required to be an optician, whereas qualifications are not needed to be a tea picker.

End-of-chapter questions

1 Football players who play for clubs in the lower league of Italian football, Serie D, are paid less than those in the top league, Serie A, because they are less skilled so fewer people are willing to pay to watch them.
2 Jobs that require high qualifications are usually paid more than those that require low, or no, qualifications as the supply of workers who can do these jobs is usually lower.
3 The key influences on demand for a worker are demand for the product s/he produces and her/his productivity.
4 Nurses in some countries are willing to work for relatively low pay because of the job satisfaction they can gain from being nurses.
5 A cut in the holidays provided by an employer is likely to reduce the supply of labour to that job as fewer people would want to do it.
6 There are a number of ways a farmer could encourage more people to work on his farm. These include raising the wage rate he pays and providing more training.
7 An increase in the pay of teachers may reduce the supply of university lecturers. This is because some university lecturers may resign in order to become teachers.
8 The wages of doctors are likely to fall if more students study medicine at university. This is because the supply of doctors will increase.

9 Some workers join trade unions in order to protect their interests. They may also hope that the trade unions will raise their wages and improve their working conditions.

10 A national minimum wage is designed to help the low-paid.

Chapter 7

Individual activities

1 a 86 years (approximately) – 52 years (approximately) = 34 years (approximately)

b Most of the countries in the World Factbook 2017 (using 2016 figures) were in the expected order with the exception of Swaziland: Japan ($41 200), Argentina ($20 100), China ($15 400), Bolivia ($7200), Ethiopia ($1900) and Swaziland ($9800).

Group activities

1 a The list should include a number of items of food. It may also include, for example, heating and transport.

b The only case when someone in absolute poverty would not be in relative poverty would be when everyone in the country lacks access to some basic necessities. As it is very unlikely that everyone in a country will be in absolute poverty, those who are will be in relative poverty. They will have less income than others in the country and so will have access to fewer goods and services.

c Italy and the UK. These two countries have the highest percentage of households who have a car, TV and internet access. Any household without a car, TV or internet access is likely to feel they cannot engage in the activities that most people in their countries are enjoying.

2 Suggested reasons may include:

- poor education
- lack of education
- low aspirations
- worse healthcare
- few contacts.

3 For instance, the Mauritian government pays a state pension to every Mauritian citizen aged 60 and over. In 2017 it paid 5450 Mauritian rupees (Rs5450) a month to those aged 60–89 years, Rs15 450 to those aged 90–99 years and Rs20 450 to those aged 100 years and above.

4 a Poverty is more of a problem in Malawi than in Germany as the average income is much lower. Malawi also has a higher percentage of children who are underweight, a smaller percentage of the population with access to clean, drinkable water and fewer years of education for its children.

b There may be some rich people in Malawi who have a higher income than some of the poor in Germany.

End-of-chapter questions

1 No, some people are rich in a poor country. The average income in Tanzania, for instance, is low but there are some rich people living in the country.

2 Someone in absolute poverty may lack food, clothing and/or housing.

3 The income of a person may remain unchanged but they may experience relative poverty if other people experience a rise in their incomes.

4 The rich, on average, live longer than the poor because they can afford better healthcare, better nutrition and better housing.

5 The old may be poor because they may not be working and they may receive low or no pension.

6 Those who have no qualifications are more likely to be poor than those with qualifications because they are more likely to be either low-paid or unemployed.

7 Improving healthcare may help to reduce poverty as it should mean that workers will lose fewer days off sick and will be more productive while at work.

8 Discrimination may cause poverty as those discriminated against may find it difficult to get a job or may be low-paid.

9 People in relative poverty are not always in absolute poverty. They will have a lower income than others in their country but they may be able to afford basic necessities.

10 Governments try to reduce poverty in order to raise the living standards of the poor.

Chapter 8

Individual activities

1 Saving per week ($): –10, 0, 30, 50, 90

Group activities

1 a, b and c, People save in case of emergencies, so that they can build up money to spend in the future and to provide financial support when they retire. Saving will tend to increase wealth and most people use their current disposable income to buy food.

2 a Increase. People will have more disposable income available to save.

b Decrease. There will be less incentive to save as the return will be lower.

c Decrease. People will have less disposable income to save.

d Decrease. People will need to save less to maintain a certain lifestyle.

e Increase. People are likely to save more as a precaution.

f Decrease. People may save less for their children's education.

g Increase. The new banks will provide people with more opportunity to save and may provide different ways of saving.

End-of-chapter questions

1 Saving may be considered to be delayed spending as it allows more spending to occur in the future.

2 The Chinese might save a lower proportion of their disposable income in the future if, for example, the price of housing falls or they become more confident about their job prospects.

3 A rise in the price of medical treatment is likely to increase savings. People may save more in case they have to pay for more expensive treatment.

4 The rich may save more than the poor because they can buy both what they want and need, and still have money left.

5 Banks are more likely to be willing to lend to the rich than the poor because they are more confident about the rich's ability to repay the loan. It also costs less per dollar lent to process a large loan than a small loan and the rich are more likely to be able to offer collateral (property that the bank can take if a loan is not repaid).

6 A fall in the rate of interest is likely to encourage borrowing as less will have to be paid for a loan.

7 If people become more optimistic about the future, they are likely to save less. They will be less concerned that they will experience a fall in income.

8 Saving at festival times is likely to fall. This is because people tend to spend more to enjoy themselves at these times.

9 A rise in saving may not be accompanied by a fall in spending if incomes are rising. In this case, people will be able to spend and save more.

10 An increase in saving may not benefit a country if it is accompanied by a fall in spending and if the lower spending results in lower output and people losing their jobs.

Chapter 9

Individual activities

1 a

Output	Average total cost ($)
1	100
2	90
3	80
4	70
5	60

b

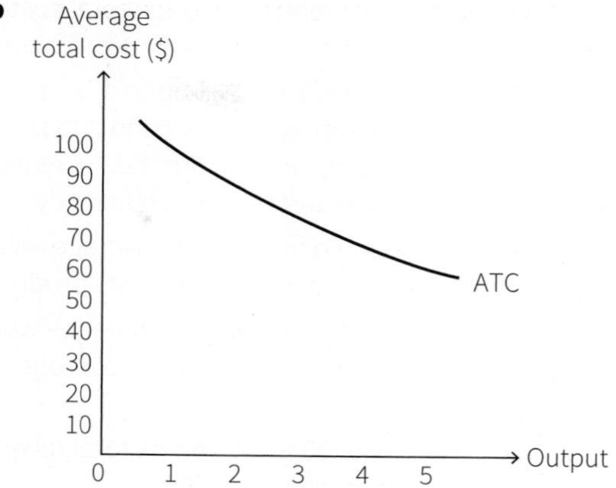

2 a \$18 000 000 (2000 × \$9000).

b \$200 (\$12 000/60).

c Profit of \$3 million (\$10 million – \$7 million).

d \$22 million (\$22 million – \$26 million = a loss of \$4 million).

Group activities

1 Costs of producing wheat: b, e, f and g.

Costs of producing train services: c, h, j and k.

Costs of building houses: a, d, i and l.

2 a It may reduce a firm's revenue if rival firms capture some of its customers. It is also possible that it may increase its revenue, if the firm responds by becoming more efficient.

b A firm could lower wages and make some of its workers redundant.

3 a Steel prices are likely to have decreased because of the fall in demand.

b A firm would expand its output if it expected that demand would increase and it would earn higher profit.

End-of-chapter questions

1 Unemployment may not rise when one firm goes out of business because those made redundant may get jobs with other firms or they may retire or go to work abroad.

2 A firm's profit will rise when its costs increase if its revenue increases by more.

3 A firm may make a loss one month, and a profit the next month, if its revenue comes in at different times and its costs, such as heating costs, vary over time.

4 Two costs of operating an airline are, for example, fuel and pilots' wages.

5 If 20 units are produced at a unit cost of \$4, total cost is \$80 (\$4 × 20).

6 If a firm becomes less efficient, its average total cost will rise.

7 A firm's average total cost will be U-shaped if, as it increases its output, its average total cost first falls and then rises. This may occur if the firm first uses its resources more efficiently and then less efficiently.

8 A firm's total revenue would fall while its average revenue remains unchanged if it sold fewer units of its product.

9 If a firm charges a price of $6, its average revenue would also be $6. This is because price is equal to average revenue.

10 If a firm makes a loss of $200 a day and its total revenue is $7500 a day, its total cost a day is $7700.

Chapter 10

Individual activities

1 **a** 59%.

b Tesco as it appears to be the largest supermarket.

Group activities

1 b, c and d are all used.

2 They are all likely to reduce average total cost and so they are all likely to enable a firm to lower its price. A lower rate of interest directly lowers one of the firm's costs. Training 200 workers will be unlikely to cost ten times that of training 20 workers. This means that average total cost will fall. A larger lorry will still only need one driver and so the cost per unit of products transported will fall.

End-of-chapter questions

1 More people are interested in gardening than in beetles. Demand for books on gardening will be greater and so more produced and sold.

2 Shoppers like low prices because they enable them to buy more.

3 A rise in average total cost is likely to increase prices. Firms are likely to raise their prices so they can cover the higher costs and still make a profit.

4 A firm may get smaller in size if demand for its products falls.

5 Mining firms are likely to be large as large capital equipment can reduce the average total cost quite significantly in this industry.

6 Improving the quality of products can help a firm grow in size as it is likely to increase demand.

7 A supplier of coffee may be prepared to sell it for a lower price per unit to a large firm with coffee shops throughout the world than to a small firm with only three coffee shops because it will expect to sell a significantly larger quantity.

8 Patients may receive better treatment in large hospitals because such hospitals are likely to have more advanced and larger medical equipment, such as operating theatres and scanning equipment, and specialised doctors.

9 A firm may be considered to be large in its own country as it may be the largest firm there. There may, however, be firms that are even larger in other countries.

10 It is uncertain whether advances in technology will improve communication between managers and workers. They will make it easier and quicker for managers to communicate with workers. There is a chance, however, that an email, for instance, may be more open to misinterpretation than a face-to-face message.

Chapter 11

Group activities

1 Air pollution: b and e.

Noise pollution: a and d.

Soil pollution: g and h.

Water pollution: c and f.

Visual pollution: i and j.

2 Private costs of air travel: a, b, e and g.

External costs of air travel: c, d and f.

3 For example, local homeowners whose homes fall in value, local residents who experience illness due to the air pollution caused by the factory and other factory-owners in the area who lose some of their staff.

4 **a** Reduce. It will be easier to dispose of the waste in a way that does not cause litter.

b Reduce. People may be more concerned about paying a higher penalty.

c Reduce. People will be better informed.

d Increase. People may be less concerned about keeping the city centre clean.

End-of-chapter questions

1 Air pollution can cause visual pollution by creating a haze.

2 Pollution is an external cost because people suffer who are not directly involved in the production or consumption of the product that causes it.

3 Farmers may cause pollution by allowing fertilisers to leak into rivers and the sea and by over-farming the land, which can reduce the fertility of the soil.

4 If social cost equals private costs, it means there are no external costs.

5 Wages paid by a shirt manufacturer to his workers are a private cost. The wages are a cost experienced by a firm that makes the decision to produce the product.

6 Third parties experience external costs.

7 Reducing private costs may increase external costs if, for example, a firm reduces the cost it experiences by dumping its waste materials on nearby common land rather than paying another firm to dispose of its waste materials.

8 Imposing taxes on firms that pollute may reduce pollution as it will give firms an incentive to cut down on the pollution they cause to avoid the fines.

9 Both social cost and social benefit are totals. They both include the effects on all those influenced by an activity.

10 Two external costs are congestion and pollution (also accidents).

Chapter 12

Group activities

1

Product	Number of litres
Almonds (1 kg)	2920
Car	81 000
Litre bottle of a soft drink	1125
Pair of jeans	9450
Smartphone	14 400
T-shirt	3150

2 a and b should increase demand for water. Tourists tend to use large amounts of water including in swimming pools. Flushing toilets uses water.

c and d should decrease demand. It takes a large amount of water to produce soft drinks and producing vegetables uses less water than producing meat.

3 a, c and d are likely to reduce the shortage. a and c would reduce demand for water. d would also reduce the waste of water and so less water would be needed. b would increase demand, as water is used to produce food.

End-of-chapter questions

1 Water is not evenly distributed among the world's population. People in some countries do not have enough water to keep themselves healthy, whereas people in other countries have more than enough so waste it.

2 Some people do overuse water whereas others do not have the opportunity to do so.

3 Price usually increases when demand exceeds supply.

4 If everyone has sufficient access to water, people will be healthier and so the quality and quantity of goods and services produced would increase.

5 The Irish government decided people would have to pay for water because they were wasting it. They had no incentive to use it carefully.

6 The economic problem will never be solved because our wants grow faster than our resources.

7 Demand for water is increasing because the world's population is rising and so there are more and more people using water and demanding products that need water to produce them. People are also getting richer. This means they use more water in, for instance, washing. Some rich families have homes with a number of bathrooms, a washing machine, a dishwasher and a swimming pool. As people are getting richer, they also buy more products that use water in their production.

8 A rise in the price of water is likely to result in a reduction in leakages from water pipes because as it is more valuable, water suppliers will be more concerned not to lose any water. Water suppliers may also earn more profit, some of which they might use to replace old water pipes.

9 A government may be reluctant to tax water as such a tax would fall more heavily on the poor.

10 Water pollution makes the problem of a shortage of water worse. This is because it reduces the supply of usable water.

Chapter 13

Individual activities

1 **a** The amount smokers have to pay to buy cigarettes.

b Asthma experienced by non-smokers.

Group activities

1 **a** Yes it is. Russia, which has the highest proportion of adults who smoke, has the lowest life expectancy. Sweden and Germany, which have the lowest proportion of adults who smoke, have the longest life expectancy.

b Differences in diet could also explain differences in life expectancy. Countries with people who have a healthy diet may also have a high life expectancy.

2 c and d are demerit goods. They are more harmful to those who buy them than they realise and they cause external costs. a and b are merit goods.

End-of-chapter questions

1 A reduction in smoking would be likely to increase life expectancy. People will be healthier.

2 A tax on cigarettes may discourage smoking as it will increase the price of cigarettes. A higher price makes people less willing and able to buy a product.

3 Two private costs of smoking are the price smokers have to pay for the cigarettes and a reduction in the health of smokers.

4 A private benefit a person may gain from stopping smoking is an improvement in her or his health.

5 Cigarettes are a demerit good as they are more harmful to the smokers than the smokers realise and because they are harmful to third parties.

6 A demerit good is more harmful than people realise while a merit good is more beneficial than people appreciate. A demerit good also causes external costs while a merit good causes external benefits.

7 A health campaign on smoking is designed to reduce demand for cigarettes. The intention is to make smokers more aware of the harm that smoking may cause to their health.

8 Increasing a tax on cigarettes may reduce tax revenue. More tax per packet of cigarettes will be raised but fewer packets will be sold and this could reduce the tax revenue the government receives from the sale of cigarettes.

9 Banning smoking in public places may reduce smoking as people will have less opportunity to smoke and they may get out of the habit of smoking.

10 Governments are more likely to ban children than adults from smoking as children may be less well informed about the harmful effects of smoking and may be more subject to peer pressure. In addition, starting smoking at a young age increases the chances of people experiencing the illnesses associated with smoking.

Chapter 14

Group activities

1 All of them. Money allows people to borrow and lend, buy and sell, save and compare the price of different products.

2 People selling goods and services are unlikely to accept eggs in payment for goods and services. Eggs do not keep for long and so cannot be used as a form of saving. Eggs are not easily portable as they can break easily.

3

1 B

China uses the yuan (also called the renminbi), Singapore uses the Singapore dollar and Thailand the baht.

2 A

China started to use paper money in approximately 806 CE. China is also the country that invented paper.

3 C

The first ATM was used in London in 1967.

4 B

A, C and D have all been used as money. Desks are not easy to carry around.

End-of-chapter questions

1 An opportunity cost of using gold as money is using the gold to make gold jewellery.

2 People accept money in exchange for goods and services as they know they can use it to purchase other goods and services.

3 Postage stamps have been used as money. For example, they were used to make small purchases in Europe during the Second World War. As the use of stamps is declining quite rapidly with the growth of other means of communication, it is unlikely that they will be used as money in the future.

4 Coins and banknotes count as cash.

5 Bartering would take time because people have to be found who not only want what you wish to exchange but also have products that you want.

6 It may be difficult to give change using barter as, for example, it is not possible to give part of an item in change.

7 The characteristic of money which allows people to give change is divisibility.

8 Durability and general acceptability are important characteristics for money to have if people are going to save it because savings may be kept for some time and to be used in the future, the money has to be acceptable to others.

9 Money being identical means that all units of the same value of the money are the same. This means that people will not mind which, for instance, US dollar they accept. They will value all the units the same.

10 Someone in India may not be prepared to accept an Australian banknote in exchange for a product because they may think that they will not be able to use it to buy other goods and services.

Chapter 15

Group activities

1 A reduction in demand for goods and services and a fall in the costs of production.

2 **a** Argentina – it had the highest inflation rate.

b Indonesia and South Africa. In these two countries, wages rose by more than prices and so people's purchasing power would have increased. People would have been able to buy less in Egypt and Turkey and the same amount in Argentina.

3 **a** It rose more slowly.

b It fell.

c 2013. The price level rose in 2014, making prices higher in 2014 than in 2013. The price level also rose in 2015. It did fall in 2016 but not enough to make the price level lower in 2016 than in 2013.The price level again rose in 2017.

d 2017. The price level rose from 2013 to 2015. It fell in 2016 but the slight decline would not have offset the rise in the earlier period and in 2017.

End-of-chapter questions

1 An inflation rate of 6% means that, on average, prices have risen by 6%.

2 While most prices rise during inflation not all prices necessarily rise during inflation. It is possible that some prices may fall.

3 The two main reasons why people's purchasing power decreases are a fall in income and a rise in prices.

4 The poor may suffer more from inflation than the rich as their income may not rise by the same percentage as inflation. The poor may, for example, have weak bargaining power.

5 Firms may raise their prices when demand increases as this may enable them to gain higher profits.

6 Increases in wages may cause inflation as it may increase firms' costs of production. This will be the case if wages rise by more than productivity. Increases in wages will also lead to higher demand which may encourage firms to raise prices.

7 If people expect a higher rate of inflation, they are likely to behave in a way that may cause prices to rise even further. They are likely to buy more products now, expecting their prices to rise, and they are likely to ask for wage rises. Higher demand and higher costs of production will raise prices.

8 Inflation may cause people to buy more products abroad if it means that the price of domestically produced products is now higher than the price of imports.

9 If a country is experiencing inflation, a government needs to know its cause so that it can take the right measures to reduce it. For example, if it finds that inflation is caused by rising total demand, it may decide to raise the rate of interest to reduce the growth in demand.

10 Training workers may reduce inflation as it can allow wages to rise without causing inflation since it should increase productivity.

Chapter 16

Individual activities

1 **a** 19.5m (6% of 325m).

b Fewer people may move from India to the USA if job opportunities increase in India. Better paid and more satisfying jobs would encourage more Indians to remain at home. Tighter immigration rules imposed by the US government may reduce the number of people from India permitted to move to the USA.

Group activities

1 **a** Just over a quarter.

b Figure 16.2 shows more immigrants into the USA are now coming from India and China. This is likely to mean that Mexico may no longer be the largest immigrant group living in the USA in 50 years' time.

2 Pull factors: a, c and d.

Push factor: b

End-of-chapter questions

1 Immigrants are moving into the country to live, whereas tourists will stay in the country only for a short time.

2 The corresponding push factor is lower wages in Mexico.

3 A fall in unemployment in Mexico is likely to reduce emigration from Mexico. Mexican workers will have a greater opportunity of getting a job and may be better paid.

4 Not all Mexican immigrants enjoy a higher living standard in the USA. Some do not find employment, some find jobs that give them less satisfaction than the jobs they did in Mexico, and some miss friends and relatives.

5 Two influences on where in the USA, Mexican immigrants may move are, for instance, job vacancies in the area and the price of housing.

6 Most countries experience both emigration and immigration. It is, however, possible that at times of war and famine, a country may only experience emigration.

7 Emigration will reduce the size of population of the country the people leave.

8 Emigration is likely to reduce the productivity in the country the people leave. This is because it is often the most enterprising and skilled workers who emigrate.

9 An increase in the quality of education in Mexico may reduce emigration of Mexicans to the USA. This is because obtaining a good education for their children is one reason people may emigrate. Better education may also increase the employment opportunities in Mexico. It is also possible however that a rise in the qualifications and skills of Mexican workers may make them more attractive to US employers.

10 More Mexicans may emigrate to countries other than the USA in the future for a number of reasons. Wages and job opportunities may increase more in other countries. The quality of education and healthcare may rise more in other countries. The US government may also place tighter restrictions on immigration from Mexico.

Chapter 17

Individual activities

1 Japan's average age was higher than Nigeria's over the period. While Japan's rose consistently, Nigeria's was relatively stable but slightly lower at the end of the period than at the start.

Group activities

1 **a** Constrictive.

b It has far more males than females (due to migrant workers).

2 a and b would increase the size of population as people would be living longer. c and d would reduce it. In the case of c, the death rate would increase. d is likely to reduce the size of the population as it may discourage some couples from having children as the cost of raising them would increase.

3 a, b and d would all help. a and d would provide the government with more revenue to support the elderly. b would reduce the amount the government has to spend on pensions. c would reduce government tax revenue and make it more difficult for the government to support the elderly. It would also increase the dependency ratio.

End-of-chapter questions

1 An ageing population may be seen as a good thing as people want to enjoy a long life. It can be seen as an indicator of improved living standards.

2 A stationary population pyramid has a rectangular shape.

3 Population pyramids taper at the top because not everyone will live to a very old age.

4 More educated women have fewer children than less educated women because they are more likely to work and want to get established in their careers. Some may decide not to have children and some may delay having children, which is likely to reduce the number of children they have.

5 A demographic time bomb is a potential population crisis. In Japan's case, it could be not having enough workers to support the elderly.

6 Two causes of a country's population getting younger could be a rise in the birth rate and net immigration. It is also possible that the death rate could rise, but most countries' death rates are falling.

7 A cut in state pensions may increase the birth rate as more couples may have children to support them in their old age.

8 A declining population may reduce a country's firms' ability to take advantage of economies of scale. This is because demand for goods and services will fall and so firms will produce less.

9 Raising the retirement age will increase government tax revenue. There will be more people working and paying income tax.

10 A rise in the retirement age in a country such as Japan may be seen as fair as people are living longer. This may mean that they will receive a state pension for the same number of years as in the past.

Chapter 18

Individual activities

1 **a** India. 9% of 510 million is 45.9 million. India has a lower unemployment rate than Afghanistan but a much higher labour force. While India had 45.9 million unemployed people, Afghanistan had 2.8 million.

b 69.12 million. If 4% of the labour force was unemployed it means that 96% were employed. So the number of people employed is 72 million × 96%.

Group activities

1 d and e. These two groups are looking for work but cannot find it. a, b and c are groups of people who are economically inactive. They are not part of the labour force as they are not seeking work.

2 Increase: a, b, c and d.

a May mean that people who have lost their jobs may not find another job quickly.

b Would reduce demand for the country's goods and services and so would lower demand for workers.

c Would make workers less productive and so less attractive to employers.

d Would make it more difficult for the unemployed in one area to move to another area where there are job vacancies.

Reduce: e. This would increase demand for the countries' goods and services and so demand for workers.

End-of-chapter questions

1 Economists do not classify the retired as unemployed as they are not seeking employment. They are not part of the labour force.

2 The labour force consists of both the employed and the unemployed. So, in this case, the size of the labour force is 40 million plus 5 million, which is 45 million.
3 The skills people need to get a job change over time as jobs change. The skills required for a nursing career, for instance, are increasing. Some nurses are now carrying out minor surgeries in some countries.
4 A variety of factors would make it easier to move from one part of the country to another. These include improvements in transport, availability of affordable housing and a similar curriculum being studied throughout the country.
5 A firm may reduce the number of workers it employs if demand for the product the firm produces falls or if it replaces some workers with machinery.
6 Living standards are likely to be higher if unemployment is lower because more people are likely to have an income that enables them to buy basic necessities. Some may now be able to afford a reasonable standard of healthcare and education. The government may also earn more tax revenue that it could spend in ways that improve people's living standards such as better housing.
7 Government spending may increase when there is unemployment as the government may spend more on benefits to help the unemployed buy basic necessities. It may also spend more on projects, such as building roads, to create jobs.
8 It may become harder for people to find another job the longer they have been unemployed because their skills may become out of date and they may lose confidence.
9 Well-educated people are less likely to be unemployed than those who are less well-educated because firms tend to want to employ people with good skills and high qualifications.
10 Cutting taxes reduces unemployment as people may spend more. This will create more demand for products and so firms are likely to recruit more workers.

Chapter 19

Group activities

1 Primary sector: e

Secondary sector: b and f

Tertiary sector: a, c, d and g

2 a, b, c and e.
3 b, c and d.

End-of-chapter questions

1 Someone might like working for the same employer for a long period of time because they will get familiar with what the work requires and will get to know the people they work with.
2 The majority of workers in most rich countries work in the tertiary sector.
3 Two advantages of working in the gig economy are wage flexibility and not having to advertise the services on offer. Workers in the gig economy can just connect to an app or website to find work.
4 It might be difficult for someone in the gig economy to get a loan to buy a house as she or he will not have a regular source of income.
5 Two possible benefits of working in the public sector are greater job security and more rights.
6 A rise in the number of females going to university is likely to increase demand for university lecturers and so raise their pay.
7 A rise in the life expectancy of their parents may reduce or increase the number of women working. Some may be less inclined to work as they may want to care for their parents themselves. Others may be more inclined to work as they may want to earn to pay for others to care for their parents.
8 Self-checkouts in supermarkets are affecting employment by reducing the number of people employed on the tills. It is, in some cases, allowing supermarkets to increase the number of other staff, such as specialist buyers.
9 A rise in life expectancy is increasing the number of people employed as doctors and nurses as older people typically require more medical treatment.
10 Regular training of workers is important as the skills required to do jobs and the jobs available are constantly changing.

Chapter 20

Individual activities

1 Trade deficit: India, Mauritius and Pakistan. In the case of these three countries, import expenditure exceeded export revenue. India had a trade deficit of $100 billion, Mauritius $2 billion and Pakistan $19 billion.

Trade surplus: China and Japan. In these two countries, export revenue was greater than import expenditure. China had a trade surplus of $395 billion and Japan had a trade surplus of $55 billion.

Group activities

1 Bangladeshi exports: b and c

Bangladeshi imports: a, d and e.

2

Country	Key export
Brazil	Sugar
Chile	Copper
China	Tea
Cote d'Ivoire	Cocoa
New Zealand	Milk
Saudi Arabia	Oil
Thailand	Rubber

End-of-chapter questions

1 Imports are products bought from abroad while exports are products sold abroad.

2 International trade encourages specialisation. Countries can concentrate on producing those products they are good at making and sell some of these to buy other products from abroad.

3 Countries do export both goods and services. For instance, India exports both gold and accounting services.

4 A fall in the price of imports will lead to a rise in import expenditure if demand for imports rises by more than the fall in price. For instance, if the average price of imports was $30 and 2,000 were sold, import expenditure would be $60,000.If the price falls to $20 and demand increases to 3,500, import expenditure would rise to $70,000

5 International trade may provide a variety of benefits to consumers. It may lead to lower prices, more choice and better quality.

6 An increase in incomes in a country may reduce that country's exports, because the country's firms may decide to sell more of its products at home.

7 A fall in transport costs is likely to increase the volume of international trade. It will be cheaper to sell products abroad and to buy products from abroad.

8 A trade deficit means that import expenditure is greater than export revenue. In contrast, a trade surplus means that a country has earned more revenue from selling exports than it has spent on imports.

9 A country's import expenditure would be $32 billion if it has a trade deficit of $8 billion and its export revenue is $24 billion.

10 The sale of tyres by a German firm to a German car producer would not appear in Germany's balance of payments as it is internal rather than international trade. It does not involve a transaction with anyone outside the country.

Chapter 21

Group activities

1 **a** India. It has an established film industry and so it is likely to have a good supply of actors and firms that provide goods and services for the film industry. It is also possible that an MNC may want to set up in a country, such as Malaysia and Myanmar, which does not have an established film industry. This is because it will not have rivals based in the country.

b Russia. It is thought that there is little gold in France and Poland. In contrast, there are already large gold mines in Russia and it is possible that more deposits of gold will be found.

c China. It has an established industry with a good supply of workers trained in the industry and supporting firms. Kazakhstan and Switzerland are landlocked countries. Being landlocked would make it difficult to test out newly built ships and impossible to launch them.

2 Allow: a and c.

a Might reduce domestic car firms' costs of production and so make them more competitive.

c Would increase the productivity of the country's banking staff and may increase employment. Some of the workers trained by the MNC may later work for the country's domestically owned banks.

Debatable: b and d.

b There is a risk that some nuclear waste may leak out and cause soil pollution and endanger lives. If, however, the MNC is a very efficient and safe firm, the country may benefit from higher employment and income.

d Domestic firms may be driven out of business by the new competition. On the other hand, they may be able to learn about the new technology. They may introduce new methods and use new machinery that may cut their costs of production. This may make them more competitive against foreign firms.

End-of-chapter questions

1 Tata is classified as an Indian MNC because its headquarters is in India.

2 If an MNC pays workers a lower wage than it pays in its home country, the workers will still benefit if the wages they receive are higher than they were earning before. For instance, a Dutch MNC may pay workers less in Indonesia than in the Netherlands, but the Indonesian workers will benefit if the wages paid by the MNC are higher than those paid by other firms in Indonesia.

3 The existence of raw materials, such as rubber, may encourage an MNC to set up in a country as it may use